TOGETHER BUT ALONE

TOGETHER BUT ALONE

WHEN

GOD

MEANS

SOMETHING

DIFFERENT

TO

YOUR

SPOUSE

DONNA ERICKSON COUCH

ST. ANTHONY MESSENGER PRESS
Cincinnati, Ohio

Book design by Jennifer Tibbits
Cover design by Mark Sullivan
Cover image © www.istockphoto.com/Dennis Oblander

LIBRARY OF CONGRESS CATALOGING-IN-PUBLICATION DATA
Couch, Donna Erickson.
Together but alone : when God means something different to your spouse / Donna Erickson Couch.
p. cm.
Includes bibliographical references.
ISBN 978-0-86716-852-5 (pbk. : alk. paper) 1. Wives—Religious life. 2. Christian women—Religious life. 3. Marriage—Religious aspects—Christianity. I. Title.
BV4528.15.C68 2008
248.8 44—dc22
2008001482

ISBN: 978-0-86716-852-5
Copyright ©2008, Donna Erickson Couch. All rights reserved.
Published by St. Anthony Messenger Press
28 W. Liberty St.
Cincinnati, OH 45202
www.SAMPBooks.org
Printed in the United States of America.
Printed on acid-free paper.
08 09 10 11 12 5 4 3 2 1

To Dana,

who walks with me
as I walk alone
on this mysterious and ordinary journey
into God

CONTENTS

ACKNOWLEDGMENTS

Writing this book has been an experience that reflects its title. I bow down in humble gratitude to all the people who gifted me with both solitude and companionship.

To my community, St. Edward the Confessor Catholic Church in Dana Point, California, you have been my sanctuary. I am grateful to Father Steve Sallot, pastor, and my wonderful faith formation staff for their kind and generous support. Mary and Liz, thanks for the laughter, hugs and morning commiserations. I also recognize the Walking Alone/Walking Together support group, especially Paula, Judy and Eva who opened their hearts to me. I also salute my friends Ellen, Jo, Mel and the many directees and confidantes who allowed me to share their stories.

To all my friends and mentors, you make walking together a delight. I acknowledge especially Joyce Cottage, my spiritual companion, for hours of patient listening. Margaret Scharf, O.P., and Mary Anne Huepper, C.S.J., at the Center for Spiritual Development in Orange, California, your encouragement inspired me. Pegge Bernecker, soul friend for life, thanks for walking with me and for insisting that I submit the proposal to Lisa Biedenbach to whom I am also grateful. Mary Noonan, my generous personal editor, I treasure our walks at Doheny Beach and your gentle and wise guidance. I give special credit to my mom and my sister, Mary Kay, for their steadfast love.

Finally, I am forever grateful to my husband, Dana, and our daughters Aimee, Elizabeth and Caitlin. Beloved mirrors of the divine, you have taught me how to love and know God by experience. May we continue this magnificent walk together.

INTRODUCTION

In 1970, at the tender age of twenty-one, I married a man who was not raised in any formal faith tradition. Further, he had no qualms about telling me that he could never see himself practicing any organized religion. Despite all the warnings from the Dominican sisters who had taught me throughout elementary and high school, I did not see his pronunciation as a problem then. Although we married in the Catholic church, I was at that time very tentative about my faith, seriously questioning exactly what had been handed to me from the cradle. I admired my husband's surety about what he believed and found a kind of freedom in it. When faced with any nagging doubts that religion might someday be an issue, I naïvely believed that our love would surely conquer all.

Throughout the many difficulties of the first seven years of marriage, I turned to God only once in a while and very quietly. There was virtually no talk between my husband and me about our inner lives, of God or of religion. While my husband was well aware of my strong Catholic roots, I never imposed any creed or doctrine on him. I didn't go to church regularly, nor did he see me praying or reading anything spiritual. Ten years into the marriage, everything changed. Mild stirrings and thoughts about God became stronger and more urgent. I eventually not only returned to my faith, but also decided to leave my chosen career as a college professor to work full-time in the Catholic church. In short, I embarked in a very big way on the spiritual journey.

No one told me while I was growing up Catholic in the early 1960s about this spiritual journey. *Journey* seemed a rather poetic word limited to book titles or rock groups. *Spiritual* conjured up an image of something very pious, restricted to priests and nuns, not relevant to the life of an average person. Despite my inclination toward the sacred (I had many numinous experiences as a child), I only considered a religious vocation briefly in junior high as I read *Maryknoll*. I always wanted to travel and held romantic ideas about what it might be like to be a missionary to Africa. However, such daydreams quickly gave way to other aspirations as I entered college in the late '60s. The spiritual journey was not, as the young people say today, even remotely on my radar screen then. A common story, God and I drifted away from each other at the altar of higher education. It took a USO (United Service Organization) tour, marriage, moving far away from home (from Minnesota to California), the birth of my first child, the tragic death of a close friend, the completion of a master's degree and dying dreams about the perfect marriage to make me start thinking seriously about God again.

Oftentimes when individuals experience an inner conversion after some years into a committed relationship, the partner is threatened by the spouse who appears on the brink of becoming a religious fanatic. A sense of mystery also troubles the one who is experiencing the divine call. A mingling of sadness and joy produces uncertainty. Questions arise like: Why me? What have I done? What do I do now? Where is this leading me? How will my relationship with God affect my spouse and family? I wrote this book for persons seeking answers to these important questions.

While I have no absolutes, I can offer decades of experiences to anyone in need of understanding and companionship. Part one explores the "walking alone" portion of the spiritual journey, a choice between stagnation and growth, longing and loneliness, solitude and community. Part two discusses the "walking together" aspects, including the mystery of relationships, children and family, friends and guides. I focus on journey as "both/and" instead of "either/or." At the end of the chapters, some suggestions for journal writing and prayer starters are included.

While I do not recommend separate faith journeys in marriage, in reality, most couples find themselves facing this dilemma at some point along the way. This book was written to give hope and support to all who desire to learn how to respond to God's call, both together and alone.

PART ONE

WALKING
ALONE

I knew right from the beginning of my marriage that if I returned to God and to the church that I was on my own. In many ways, I was glad of this. The thought of returning to the Catholic church filled me with anxiety. I had decried it many times to my husband and to friends who were also "fallen away." Admitting that I was wrong seemed like a distasteful plate of humble pie. Moreover, I wasn't sure I wanted to return to the rigidity, the rules, the doctrines I still grappled with as an adult. Could I even be a good Catholic? I certainly did not want to be one of the hypocrites that I criticized and used as an excuse for why I left in the first place. I certainly did not want to publicly announce to my husband and friends that I was returning to the faith and then fall away from it again. So I did what I always did when I was confused about something—I began to read.

First I went to the nearest bookstore and checked out the religion and spirituality shelves. I was surprised to find so many books about the subject. I began with C.S. Lewis. He was not a Catholic, but he was an intellectual who had thought long and hard about God before converting to Christianity. After devouring several of his books, I stumbled upon Thomas Merton's *The Seven Storey Mountain* and had what I would later learn to call, "an epiphany moment."[1] I was fascinated with Merton's combination of rational and emotional experience that took him from atheism to being a Trappist monk in an astonishingly short length of time. His beautiful description of divine encounters on the street corners of Louisville was touching and compelling. The concept of spiritual journey began to take root in me. I was pleased to learn that the experience was interior and meant for anyone who desired it, not just the clergy or religious.

My awakening to the possibility of spiritual growth gave me the courage to forge ahead. The silent retreat to an interior sanctuary was enticing. Many mornings I would rise early, read my books, write in my journal, take a walk and just float on the sweetness emanating from a new way of being. At first I thought maybe my journey could happen without anyone really noticing. I didn't think I needed to tell my husband or friends or anyone else about it. At the same time, many questions came up that I could not answer.

I constantly asked myself whether or not this journey was really for me. Without my partner's support, I was plagued with uncertainty and confusion. I balked at the proposition of blind faith, but I also knew that rational arguments would only take me so far. I recognized somewhere inside that the journey would require a leap, a giant trust, a commitment to a path for which I had no map or explanations. However, as I sat in the pews each Sunday by myself, I felt helplessly alone. Was there no one to walk with me? The ubiquitous presence of couples and families was a source of envy and sadness. I had no idea with whom to talk about my baffling situation. Many more times than I can relate, fear overwhelmed and sickened me. Yet, simultaneously, a growing love for God pushed me onward into the hope that walking alone had many lessons to teach me about relationships.

CHAPTER ONE

GROWTH
AND
STAGNATION

While cleaning out the attic recently, I stumbled upon a dusty, brittle cardboard box containing many forgotten mementos. Nestled inside one old manila envelope were the many yellowing cards received from friends and relatives when we married. Looking at them made me feel like I was in one of the antique shops I frequently haunt. Wedding cards in 1970 were, for the most part, sentimental caricatures of traditional marriage roles. Gold-trimmed edges, smiling cherubs, doves circling bells, rose bouquets and couples looking longingly into one another's eyes echoed the themes of eternal love and happiness. The simple, rhymed verses presented a more innocent time:

> As you start your life together
> You are wished life's finest things
> And all the deep contentment
> That a perfect marriage brings
> May you find in days ahead
> Your dearest dreams come true
> And that your life together
> Brings much happiness to you.

As I read them, I recalled my past thoughts that the cards and gifts sincerely sent from these good-hearted, decent people were symbols of rather strongly held cultural views of the ideal marriage. I was a bit cynical then, doubtful that any of the senders really understood love. Married folks I knew at that time didn't seem very happy. Living together was beginning to be the preferred arrangement for some couples, and many women were choosing not to marry based on feminist principles. Despite all this, I felt absolutely certain that our marriage would be vastly different. After all, our unique love story held immense promise. We met in Athens, Greece. I was entertaining in a USO traveling show from the University of Minnesota, and he was stationed there in the army. On our first date we explored the Parthenon by moonlight and walked hand-in-hand through the acropolis. After a whirlwind of daily letters, long-distance phone calls and cross-country flights, we married in my hometown in Minnesota about eight months later. We moved to California (his home state) immediately. When the romantic dust settled, the lessons about the reality of marriage began.

DIALECTICAL TENSIONS

My naïveté about married love was shattered when I realized that I had married someone who had a driving need for independence while at the same time wanting me, our marriage and our home. He loved to play golf for five or six hours every weekend, took his time coming home from work each night and enjoyed watching virtually any sporting event on television. I had never played golf, expected that my husband would come home to my arms immediately after work and was not interested in televised sports. I wanted him to go to live theatre and movies, to shop with me for household items and groceries and to work with me on projects around the house on weekends. He fell asleep during plays, only liked action movies and hated shopping and projects. Without the benefit of family close by or any support network, I learned my first lesson about walking alone in marriage as we struggled with what experts call "dialectical tensions." These tensions arise whenever individuals in a relationship hold incompatible goals. Often, the tensions are experienced internally and are not verbalized well. The struggle to manage these tensions frequently creates powerful dynamics, embodying a constant polarization between integration versus separation, stability versus change and expression versus privacy. How we manage these tensions either enhances or destroys the relationship.[1]

INTEGRATION VERSUS SEPARATION

Most of us spend our young lives looking for our soul mate, someone to connect with who will make us feel complete so that we can settle into a sense of familial love that will last forever. Union with a partner drives us powerfully, producing constant thoughts and actions centered on the other. The sense of self temporarily evaporates into another reality, the life of "we" the couple. Personal needs willingly sublimated, desires of fostering the new relationship dominate and dizzy us until this honeymoon period ends. After the initiating and intensifying stages pass, we soon settle into a new pattern, one that will continue to confound us throughout the life of the relationship. While we still yearn for intimacy, we simultaneously find ourselves not willing to sacrifice our entire identity. Our need to connect and our need to be independent create the integration versus separation dialectic that often forces people into thinking that the relationship is over. We want to be close but at the same time we seek independence. Couples often express discontent when one wants more autonomy than the other. Sometimes, the one who wants less independence interprets this need as a rejection.

This tension made me wonder more than twice why my partner wanted to get married in the first place. "Why don't you want to spend more time with me?" was the question that I constantly asked at the beginning of my marriage. His answer was always adamantly the same: "Of course I want to spend time with you. We're married, aren't we?" Obviously, we saw independence and integration differently! I soon realized that if we were going to stay in this commitment, then we needed to negotiate a climate of respect for each others' needs. Rather than harbor negative feelings, I decided to take his desire for independence as an invitation to develop my own sense of autonomy. I went back to college, purchased season tickets to the theatre with a close friend and learned to enjoy doing some projects on my own. Meanwhile, my husband and I established a dinner date every Friday night and planned special times to attend sporting events and concerts with musicians we both liked. These early compromises, I firmly believe, established the foundation for what would come later, namely, a mutual respect for the individual journey of faith.

STABILITY VERSUS CHANGE

Yet another potentially polarizing dialectic encompasses the need for stability versus change. We feel comfortable when we can predict what our partner might do or feel. However, a stagnation of the relationship can also happen if we are too stable and conventional. "He's as comfortable as an old shoe," a woman told me when I asked about her relationship with her husband. She communicated with resignation that while she liked the feel of the footwear, the style was now tedious.

On the other hand, we feel equally restless when our partner changes too much. "I don't know who she is anymore," was the comment of one partner. He lamented that spirituality had so possessed his spouse that even her style of clothing had changed. She wouldn't go to the same movies or watch the same television shows they had always shared. The story on the other side was equally frustrated. "He wants me to be the person he married twenty-five years ago and that's just not possible." Change to one person is positive growth, to the other, relational death. Acknowledgment and discussion of these tensions gives rise to hope if both husband and wife are willing to sacrifice.

DISCLOSURE VERSUS PRIVACY

Similarly, the tension between disclosure and privacy may become problematic. There are times when we feel the need to verbalize every thought to our partner including every dream, secret, activity, longing. Chattering away about everything and anything, while typical and necessary at the beginning of a relationship, eventually changes when the need for privacy emerges between people. We discover that there are many things we should not reveal for one reason or another. Honest talk about some topics may cause unnecessary hurt—"You don't have the figure to wear that swimsuit." Revealing dark moods that surely will pass may upset the other's sense of immediate joy— "I'm glad you're having a great day. This has been the worst day of my life!" Ideas that are not well formed within us may confuse and trouble the other: "I'm thinking about quitting my job and joining the FBI." The belief that love relationships should contain no secrets nor private thoughts and feelings is a myth that has needlessly destroyed many a good relationship. Learning to respect the boundaries of privacy and disclosure fosters, not tears down, the sense of love and intimacy that develop between people.

The expression of private thoughts and feelings about God is a good example. Telling stories about spiritual experiences sometimes causes others to misunderstand or undermine what is only known deeply in the heart. Numerous persons in spiritual direction tell me that when they try to talk to their partners about spirituality it does not go well. One woman said that her husband looked at her like she was from another planet when she shared with him her sense that angels were in the room. "I seriously thought he was going to have me committed that day!" she exclaimed with great regret. The question posed to me is always the same: Do I have to tell my partner about these unexplainable phenomena? Is it wrong to withhold these life-altering perceptions of God's presence? The answer is always the same. No! There is a time for disclosure and a time for privacy. Finding the appropriate time to act on each of them fosters a healthy love relationship.

NAMING THE REALITY

Dialectical tensions exist within all relationships, even the best and most intimate. Naming their existence right from the beginning is a huge step in overcoming the tendency to bolt when they arise. Recently, my middle daughter, Elizabeth, married. As part of their celebration, they wanted to light the unity candle. The ritual goes like this: three candles are placed in a holder. The two outer candles represent the two individuals, the two families. The middle candle represents the new union they are creating. At the beginning of the ceremony, my daughter wanted the mothers to light the outer candles. After the vows, they would light the center candle together as a couple. A serious conversation about whether or not to extinguish the outside candles arose. What was being communicated? They soon decided that the symbolism of leaving the three candles burning would remind everyone that there are two important needs in marriage, the need to become a couple and the need to remain separate individuals. Recalling this simple action throughout the many challenges of marriage helps reinforce that important reality.

Dialectical tensions comprise what I call the "walking alone" part of being and remaining in an intimate relationship with another person. Facing the reality of individualism aids in understanding how to manage spirituality when the one we love does not understand or agree. The tensions described above need to be thought of as "both/and" rather than "either/or" propositions. We are autonomous *and* connected; we are highly revealing *and* private; we love our stability *and* we love change. Pursuing a spiritual life is no different. When one person wants God at the center of life and the other is ambivalent, a self-proclaimed agnostic or atheist, a conflict exists that can make communication challenging. Unfortunately, many couples allow these tensions to tear them apart.

A CASE IN POINT

Finola, an intense and serious woman in middle age, came to me in tears one day because her husband of twenty years had called her a religious fanatic, objecting loudly to her desire to see a spiritual director. She said he had withdrawn from her emotionally, giving her the silent treatment. I suggested to her that perhaps other troubles were brewing and that he was only using her faith as a scapegoat.

Finola disagreed because when confronted, he always responded the same way—she had changed too much; he didn't want to be married to someone who seemed to be "having an affair with God." For many months, I did not see Finola at church, and she did not contact me for spiritual direction. Friends told me that she had decided to curtail her intense pursuit of a spiritual life because her marriage was in danger. After a year's absence, Finola asked me for some guidance about a troubling dream.

In the dream, Finola was swimming in a lake full of green algae that kept getting thicker and heavier with each stroke. Treading water, the sensation of drowning came upon her as she struggled to stay above water. Suddenly, she felt a tremendous force—maybe a shark?—pulling her down into the deep. Looking up through the verdant slime, she saw a small orb of white light far away but no amount of kicking and screaming could bring it closer. She awoke in a panic. As Finola described the dream to me, her troubled eyes gazed into the distance, her beautiful face constricted with the pain of remembrance. Together we walked back through the many symbols of this powerful dream. Finola knew what her subconscious was telling her. Giving up her interior faith life was choking off other parts of her life. We talked about many subjects in the subsequent weeks. The underlying theme came back over and over. When her spiritual practice was sacrificed, Finola felt like she was dwelling at the bottom of a cavern, stagnating in the muck and unfiltered water. Fear had paralyzed her. She had anxiety attacks in line at the grocery store. She was now on antidepressants. Her resentment, not her faith, was killing the love between her and her husband.

Nightmare fears often bring about transforming results. Finola decided one day to choose a path of growth for herself and for her husband. She went home to negotiate a new relationship, setting up a boundary that respected her expressions of faith and his decision not to participate. The fear that had gripped her life slowly began to fade as she acknowledged her interior longing once again for a faith beyond church on Sundays.

LETTING GO OF FEAR

Finola, and many others of us who spiritually walk alone, must renegotiate the "rules" of intimate relationships when a calling for God echoes within us. More than simply agreeing not to talk about religion, we also must let go of the fear that an enhanced spirituality will destroy the delicate balance of marriage. Loving another person intimately means a constant redefinition of the relationship as the years go on. At the heart of such fear is often the familiar comfort of knowing who I am, who you are and who we are as a couple. Sometimes this security, dysfunctional or healthy as it might be, possesses and grips us tightly. Despite all the shortcomings, it is often easy to convince oneself to just let it go and not risk upsetting the apple cart.

When fear has evolved into a comfortable pattern, we think it is easier to dwell in the stagnated place than to allow God to take us to unknown destinations that may seemingly dismantle the foundations we have built. Ultimately, we learn to name this fear as a fallacy. Relationships are meant to continually grow and evolve over time in new ways that allow both the couple and the individual room for satisfying identities that are both together and separate. Lesson number one: It is normal to feel torn by these conflicting dialectics.

Growth and development takes place in many different arenas over the course of years, not just in the spiritual realm. The life of the relationship must be able to hold the tensions of inevitable change.

Like any other life issue, spirituality requires discipline, time and commitment to develop into anything truly meaningful. A relationship with God takes the same type of care required of any other worthwhile endeavor. Conversely, spirituality stagnates and dies on the vine without intentional effort. Perhaps this seems obviously simplistic. However, for those who face the decision to grow in the faith without the support of a loved one, such a notion brings consternation. Fear of the unknown consequences of spiritual growth poses multiple dilemmas about personal identity and lifestyle changes. How much time will this require? How can I integrate the principles of faith without alienating my mate? Will God come between us? The recurring sense that conversion does not come without some price to pay can make one pause. The sense of imminent martyrdom of the self and of the relationship often thwarts the journey before it begins. Yet the need for communion with God propels us on and, if we are able to hold the dialectical tensions maturely and wisely, we learn that it is not God who comes between people or alienates us from anyone. We do that on our own by not spending the time to discern how we will communicate and live out our spiritual journey. Some practical steps may be helpful here.

GOING PUBLIC

The first step in the commitment to growth is the ultimate decision to go public with your plans for spiritual growth. No, you don't have to make a public confession or take out an advertisement in the newspaper. However, you do have to let your partner know how you

are feeling about God and your need to live out of spiritual principles. This may cause great trepidation at first. Take some time to listen to your own fears. Every feeling provides an opening for prayer.
Communicate your misgivings with God and ask for whatever you
need to accomplish the first step. Courage, timing, the right words
and an open heart are all fair requests. Meditate on how you want
the encounter to go, what you will say, how the other will react.
Picture a perfect outcome. Then set a time to talk when nothing else
will distract. All of these guidelines will facilitate a smoother
encounter and a sense of peace within your own soul. My own story
is a good example.

When spirituality, my sense of coming home again to my faith,
was all so new and deliciously innocent, I wasn't ready at first for
anyone (especially the one I loved) to ruin it for me. So I waited
quite a while to broach the subject. This was easy because my husband didn't really notice what I was reading, and I did not initiate
conversation about anything remotely spiritual. There were times,
however, when I wondered why he never noticed, so big was the
swelling inside of me, the love for God that seemed to be pouring
from every part of me. But he didn't. I put off telling him for
months. It wasn't until I found a nearby church community and had
gone to the sacrament of confession that I finally summoned the
courage to tell him.

The priest who heard my confession was, quite unwittingly, the
catalyst for the eventual confrontation. I was naturally nervous and
quite shameful about my past. I tried to confess as many sins as I
could remember in the decade I had stayed away, and I was prepared
to take whatever guilt the priest might dish out. I thought I deserved

as much. However, after a wonderful dialogue and the first absolution I had received in more than ten years, Father Matt smiled and welcomed me home with open arms. Tears of joy streamed down my face, and I remained for a long time on my knees, lost in a sea of gratitude. Soon confession time was over, and as I walked out of the church, I found myself face to face with the same priest who had been so kind and gentle with me. We had a casual conversation about what I did for a living (I was a professor at the local community college), family and children. I mentioned off-handedly that my husband was an avid golfer and saw the priest's eyes light up. Father Matt was new to the parish, he said, and looking for a golf partner. Would my husband be interested? The prospect of a priest playing golf with my husband was so astonishing that I didn't have a plausible excuse. "Sure," I mumbled, as he took down our name and phone number. I had been looking for signs and this was a big one. If a priest was going to be calling our house, asking for my husband, now was the time to go public. After prayer and practicing what I wanted to say, I made a date night complete with dinner and candlelight. I remember distinctly sitting at our dining room table, heart pounding and voice low, the way he looked at me, expecting the worst when I finally said I had something important to discuss.

Telling my husband turned out to be not as cataclysmic as I thought, the anticipation far worse than the actual encounter. He simply shrugged his shoulders and said it was fine with him but quickly added that he would not be a participant. His thoughts on the subject had not changed over the years. When I told him that I wanted to bring our daughter (our only child at the time) into the faith, he seemed unfazed. Again, no problem, as long as he was not expected to walk along with us. Fighting back a few tears, I told him I understood and would honor his personal decision. I had not expected anything different. Emotionally, I had just tasted my first sip of bittersweet holy wine. Full of poignant sadness, I had nonetheless taken the first step on a new journey, alone, within our marriage. More than a little scared about what this might do to our relationship, I made a resolution to follow my heart and, for the first time, trust what I had never dared to trust before—I really was not alone. God was with me.

In the subsequent weeks, I told my closest friends about my inner conversion. Most of them were pleasantly surprised and expressed happiness for me. Some were puzzled and some were downright challenging, looking at me like I had just told them I wanted to become a nun. Meanwhile, Father Matt and my husband did play golf together. What's more, they became great friends! I thought for a while that their friendship would change Dana's worldview and that he would eventually embark on the spiritual journey. Although that little dream never materialized, I still believe to this day that God had telegraphed a significant message to me when I finally "went public." I was not to worry. Getting my own spiritual life together was all that was required. This included loving my partner in a manner befitting God by respecting his freedom not to participate.

FAITH DEVELOPMENT

The first step of going public, as I mentioned before, produces anxiety. According to all the saints, mystics and many theologians, well it should. Before us looms the strange and mysterious adventure of traversing holy ground. As much as I read about it, thought about it, prayed about it and desired the thought of it, the experience of living

21

it out differed greatly from any abstraction. The ordinary, gritty events of everyday life contain important spiritual lessons that recycle day after day, year after year, in a predictable pattern of growth and development. Realization and acceptance that spiritual growth would be an ongoing and ever-changing phenomenon comprises the next step of the journey.

Hungry for knowledge, I dove into the spiritual classics with a tiger-like ferocity, reveling in the freedom of not having to hide my spiritual life anymore. What I learned immediately from countless spiritual writers was a lesson that continues to unfold. That is, we never fully arrive at our destination—union with God—here on earth. Rather, we will continue to move from points of stagnation into growth as we journey through life. Father Ronald Rolheiser calls the first part of the spiritual life "essential discipleship."[2] During this time, we strive, as I surely did, to just get our lives together and come back home again after the tumultuous prodigal years. Characteristic of this time, the great struggle to learn what it means to live a life grounded in God continues. We must constantly wrestle with the chaos that dwells innately within the human soul. Over time, the initial phase passes and, according to Rolheiser, a period of "generative discipleship" arises, the time when we are called to sacrifice our whole lives for the sake of others. What this means individually is unique. No longer do we struggle constantly with morals, who to marry, what we want to do with the rest of our lives. Instead, with these choices in the background, we tackle God's will, the complex discernment of how to substitute selfishness with altruism. Eventually, after many years of selfless giving, we embrace the "radical discipleship" of old age that prepares us for the ultimate homecoming into God's eternal promise.[3]

James Fowler, another expert on faith development, tells us specifically what those stages encompass throughout the span of an entire lifetime. Beginning in utero, he says, we have a propensity for God that drives us immediately after we are born. Our capacity to grow spiritually enlarges as we mature from concrete operations to abstract thinking. Throughout young adulthood, we make intentional choices that either draw us into a deeper search for the divine or keep us forever childish or adolescent in our understanding of anything spiritual.[4] In essence, a ninety-year-old woman could perpetually hold the religious beliefs of a small child regardless of whether or not she practices any faith. She may look wise and mature on the outside, but her spiritual growth has never progressed.

Moving from one stage to another is a very solitary experience. While others may accompany us, they are peripheral to the individual soul's development. No two people, no matter how close the bond, ever develop at the same rate or in the same way. As in my case, realizing this important truth and making peace with it was an enormous step. Knowing that our separate journeys were a natural part of the quest for God gave me the courage to face many other challenges of walking alone.

CONCLUDING REFLECTIONS

Revisiting the attic and finding the wedding cards that warm spring day affirmed what had taken thirty-plus years to fully realize. When we love another person, we face a sea of unknowns, including a critical lesson about growth and stagnation. If we accept God's invitation to live life to the fullest, then we are faced with an ongoing process of pondering, holding and managing the dialectical tensions that come with intimate relationships. It means letting go of the fear that paralyzes us to remain on the periphery of life. It means going public, admitting to the ones we love that commitment to God will mean commitment to growth. It means embracing the surprises that await us as we progress through the many stages of faith development. Whether it means a vibrant, abundant life or a life of anxious desolation, the choice is yours to make alone. Whatever choice you make, the result produces rippling effects that go out like concentric circles in a pond, touching everyone who dares to accompany you on the journey.

CHAPTER TWO

LONGING, LONELINESS AND LOVE

The peace that came after my recommitment to the faith and subsequent "coming out" soon faded as I began the hard work of living out my spiritual principles on a day-to-day basis. At home with my books, journals, tapes and newfound spiritual music, I was relatively centered. When my children and I went off to church on Sundays, it was another story. Just as pregnant women see other pregnant women everywhere, all I could see during Sunday Mass were couples—smiling couples who looked newly engaged; couples with children in tow; couples with extended family members; older couples who still looked delightfully in love. Most poignant of all for me were the couples who received Communion with their arms around each other. As I watched them, my heart longed for something I knew I might never have with my spouse. A new yet familiar loneliness began to engulf me as I struggled to imagine my life with God at the center.

I did not know then that longing and restlessness never leave, regardless of whether or not the one I love shares my spiritual journey. Even though I had studied the egocentric predicament in basic philosophy class in college, I naively thought that getting married would somehow erase (or at least greatly reduce) the nagging feeling of loneliness that I had always felt throughout my life. I remember feeling it as a child struggling to get attention and love. I remember feeling it as a teenager awkwardly trying to find someone to be my best friend, to dance with, to date and notice me. I remember feeling it intensely when I moved away from home to go to the University of Minnesota in Minneapolis. I was suddenly the proverbial small fish in a big pond. Even though my best friend roomed with me, I spent many hours feeling desperately alone as I struggled not only to succeed in college but also to support myself financially. The love I held for the theater and my driving need to make it as an actress kept feelings of despair from overwhelming me.

My short theatrical career was a source of great joy, and I recall it with a smile. However, in a stark way, it also reinforced my feelings of loneliness. While the audience might love you, the critics rarely did and neither did the other actors who were competing with you for a choice role. By the time the auditions for the USO show were completed and I was one of the five students chosen, I had simultaneously received a big dose of both affirmation and alienation. I landed the part but lost jealous friends in the process, including an important boyfriend who couldn't stand sharing my triumph. I was only twenty years old, but I felt like I was eighty at times. Given the state of my wounded soul, it wasn't surprising that I jumped quickly into marriage when a strong man came into my life who adored me and wanted to take care of my every need.

The forlorn feelings went away for a while in the periodic moments of utter bliss when I was in his arms and our life was ascending. However, since I had moved far away from family and friends when we married, the lonely feelings returned as I sought to establish a new home in a new state with new people. It took a while to adjust even though I made friends rather easily. Meanwhile, like so many of us, I denied the isolating feelings whenever anyone asked how I liked married life in California.

Loneliness can be seriously destructive to relationships. We either become very possessive of what we have or we sink into the blues that can block the beauty and joy of being in the present moment. Driving us into premature and irresponsible decisions, loneliness is often the cause of great unhappiness, evidenced by the many people who fall into unhealthy relationships with people they mistakenly think love them. Fired with need, some of us go from one relationship to another, never finding what we are longing for at the core of our beings. We look for love "in all the wrong places," as the song goes, endlessly searching for the ideal mate to take away an innate condition we cannot escape. This fire to find someone can burn us down to nothing, yet, ironically, that same fire also holds the greatest potential for transformation. A great deal depends on how we choose to handle the challenge.

First and foremost, we need to realize that loneliness, like no other condition, pressures us to take the risk of loving another person. We might get burned but at least we know what the fire was like. That love then can draw us into greater creativity and empathy for others. Inside the intense moments of ecstasy, we get our first real taste of what it means to say that "God is love." The force that draws us so powerfully toward union with another person inebriates us with joy and the loneliness subsides. We have no control over the soaring and piercing feelings that surprise and drive us. The lingering sense of mystery, that all is gift, pervades us. We are enticed to risk again with other loving relationships. In doing so, we enter and can participate in the fullness of God's presence, available to us all the time. We are then ready to begin the intimate journey of becoming a truly great lover because healthy union with others constitutes what we ultimately desire: union with God.[1]

The decision to live out of this spiritual principle most certainly put a new spin on the experience of loneliness for me. However, I continued to struggle with the uncertain reality of what it meant to walk alone with a vision that was not shared with my partner. During the early part of my spiritual awakening, I tiptoed through Saint Augustine's writings with great caution. Once I got past his archaic language, he taught me a valuable spiritual lesson about the human condition. I found great comfort as I read: "You have made us for yourself, Lord, and our hearts are restless until they rest in you."[2] After hours reading the mystical writings of John of the Cross, Teresa of Avila and many other commentaries, I learned that the kind of "rest" that they described with such eloquence was going to take some time, maybe even a whole lifetime.[3] I knew I needed to accept that challenge and continue to seek spiritual wisdom from the role models and stories of my faith tradition.

MARY'S STORY

As I searched for inspiration from the many spiritual women of our tradition, I began to think again about Mary, the Mother of God, something I had not done since I was very young. A little book came my way that I still reread every Advent. *The Reed of God* by Caryll Houselander taught me a valuable truth about how to manage the loneliness within the human spirit.[4] Houselander's book suggests that

Mary's universal appeal comes from the parallel experience we share with her. For example, we are born, like Mary, unaware of God's favor. At some point, when we are pure and open enough (virginal), we are awakened to a choice that, if we say yes, will impregnate us with the capacity to birth a great love into the world. We don't know what we are getting into when we say yes. However, when we do, the love transfigures everyone and everything. Predators try to destroy the beauty and we suffer greatly trying to nurture and keep that love alive. Sometimes it feels as though swords are piercing our hearts but in the end, the love we have protected throughout all the pain transforms us, body, mind and spirit.

Knowing that even the Mother of God was not spared feeling alone on her journey was immensely helpful to me. Granted, her story differed from mine in a lot of ways. Joseph seemed to be the perfect mate for her. They shared the same religion, and I get the sense that he was devout in his practice. Yet, his choice to take Mary as his wife was not without its problems. Their marriage began with turmoil and secrets and certainly did not get off to a good start. Yet they persevered through judgments, misunderstanding and maybe even their own confusion. Since Joseph isn't mentioned in Scripture after Luke's infancy narrative, it has been traditionally taught that he died before Jesus' public ministry. Again, Mary was left to find her way alone in a culturally patriarchal world. She had much to teach me about the walking alone part of my journey as did my daughter.

CONNECTING WITH SIGNS, SYMBOLS AND STATUES

Round about pondering Mary's story, I felt a desire to bring religious images into my heretofore secular home. I frequently came across many statues and sacred pictures when I scoured my favorite antique shops. They never held much appeal before, but suddenly I was fascinated. For at least the first two years of my spiritual walk, I never purchased any such articles. I couldn't imagine what my husband would say if I brought one home. And then, where would I put it? No room seemed appropriate. I did, however, begin to collect a few gold crosses on chains, rosary beads, medals that I hid in drawers. As is frequently the case, it took my child's burgeoning faith to bring a religious image into our home and to dispel some of the loneliness I was feeling within our family.

My oldest daughter, Aimee, was eight years old when I openly began to practice spirituality. She possessed then (and still does today, at thirty-six), a sweet openness and acceptance of the sacredness of life. She never questioned me when I told her that I wanted to have a relationship with God. I remember how her little face lit up as she enthusiastically asked me if she could have that, too. Aimee embraced the faith as though it had been a part of our lives from the beginning. What's more, she talked about God endlessly not only to me but also to her dad, who listened to her ramblings without comment. When we attended church together, Aimee was the one who asked me if we couldn't please have a cross, a picture or statue in our home. I told her we would someday when we found just the right piece. I was stalling about making a visual statement in our home. Interestingly, the decision was made for me very soon afterward.

On a Tuesday afternoon in May, when I went to the parish school building to collect Aimee after her religious education class, I was told that the class was over in the church taking a tour. Aimee was very excited to show me a large statue of Our Lady of Fatima sitting on a pedestal near the sanctuary. "Isn't she beautiful?" she whispered in my ear. The statue was creamy white with gold leaf trim. Mary's hands were folded, her face gently smiling, her gaze both penetrating and soft. I had never seen the statue before and learned later that it belonged to the Blue Army, a Marian group devoted to praying for world peace. Honestly, I was a bit disarmed by what this image represented to me, a very traditional leftover from the pre–Vatican II church of my childhood. Some vague negative feelings about the past stirred in me, but I feigned enthusiasm for my daughter's sake. The following Sunday, Aimee was delighted to show me an invitation in the church bulletin from the Blue Army to host the statue in the homes of parishioners. "Mom, please can we have Mary come to our house?" The moment of truth had come. How could I say no?

As the scheduled Tuesday approached, I did not know how to tell my husband that a four-foot-tall statue of the Virgin Mary would be with us for a week. I need not have worried. Aimee told him over dinner that very night. "Dad, did you know that Mary is coming to our house tomorrow?" This got his attention, but he thought she meant my sister, Mary, who lives in Minnesota. "Mary's coming?" he asked, surprised that I had not told him that we would be having company. "Ah, not that Mary," I replied. Aimee continued to chatter away about how the statue looked and her plans to show it to her friends.

"It's only for a week, and Aimee will keep it in her room," I told him later, apologetic and embarrassed about the fuss our daughter was making over a statue. "Whatever," was the only response I got from him, but I could tell that he wasn't all that pleased.

When we picked up the statue, bundled in a blue quilted blanket tied with beige grosgrain ribbons, Aimee quivered with pleasure.

"She looks like she's taking a nap," she remarked, as we carried the statue to the car. I felt a bit like I was smuggling contraband out of an art gallery. At home, when I headed for her room, Aimee objected. She wanted to put Mary on the fireplace, the first thing you see when you come in our front door. Try as I might to persuade her differently, she was stubbornly adamant, which was not characteristic of her at all. I could have overpowered her, but I did not have the heart to extinguish her sweet delight. So together we placed Mary on the hearth in all her glory. I watched as my excited daughter went out and picked every flower in sight and festooned them around the base of the statue. I let her arrange my best scented candles in a pious arc at her feet. We lit each one and recited the entire prayer card that accompanied the statue. Silently, I stared at Mary as I reveled in my Aimee's innocence. A cry from my heart rose up into my churning and longing chest: May your presence bring us together, not apart.

That night, when my husband came home from work, he didn't really have a chance to ease into our living room turned Marian shrine. Aimee ran to the door and led him directly to the statue (as if he could have missed it). "Wow, that's something! She's really...big!" That was all he could say, looking at me with a smile and obviously seeing how much this meant to our daughter. My heart soared as I looked back at him. We needed no explanations then. We had turned a corner somehow. My prayer for him to acknowledge my interior journey was answered but not in the way I had envisioned. Acceptance had happened in a little way, without words, without theological reflections, without arguments.

Throughout the whole week, Aimee paraded all our neighbors into the living room to visit the statue. By then, she knew the story of Fatima and wasn't at all shy about telling the details. Listening from the kitchen in the middle of preparing dinner, my thoughts returned again to Mary of Nazareth, a woman, just like me, who probably cut vegetables and worried about her child eating enough protein. I thought about her sweeping the floor, doing the laundry, lying down beside a man who did not understand but who had accepted anyway. Yes, it was true. Her story was and is my story. Everything that happened to her was happening to me in the very simple and ordinary events of my life.

We hosted the statue in our home many times in subsequent years. Aimee especially wanted Our Lady with us during the Christmas holidays when they let us keep her for two weeks. After her two sisters were born and Aimee was a teenager, the three of them faithfully carried on the tradition. My husband quietly accepted its presence, our daughters' growing devotion, and the many icons that slowly began showing up on the walls of every room in our house.

THE PASCHAL MYSTERY

Resolving the human condition of loneliness faces everyone, not just people who walk alone in faith. How we choose to respond to this reality shapes and molds the relationships we choose to draw into our lives. Looking at Mary in her humanity, as a woman not so different from me, was very helpful. However, perhaps the deepest insights I had about longing, loneliness and love came gradually to me as I pondered the paschal mystery with seekers in RCIA (Rite of Christian Initiation for Adults).

Not long after joining the community at St. Edward the Confessor Church, I was invited to become a catechist. After my initial incredulity that anyone wanted me to teach religion, I embarked on a grueling adventure. While I was confident of my expertise as a college professor, I could not imagine teaching anything except the speech communication classes I so loved. But, since no one had ever asked me to talk about God in the classroom before, I took the request as yet another sign that God was trying to tell me something. Out of my comfort zone, I was very resistant when asked to substitute teach in a junior high school session. However, saying yes was a promise I had made to God when the journey began, and so I taught the class, albeit not very well. One experience led to another and soon I was teaching confirmation preparation to high school students on a regular basis.

In the process, I became closely acquainted with our taciturn, intellectual Scottish pastor, Father Louis F. Knight. To this day, I do not know what prompted our friendship except to say that he took an interest in my credentials as a college instructor. We had long talks about my thesis on phenomenology and about his dissertation on collegiality. Later, he requested that I instruct an adult inquiry class for individuals seeking conversion to Catholicism. Again, I was riddled with doubts. Teaching high school students was an ordeal but teaching religion to adults was another matter altogether. Why me? What did I know? My religious education ended my senior year in high school. Father Knight assured me that I could do it because I was "a professional." Despite my fears, I was intrigued, knowing that what you teach, you end up learning yourself a hundred times over. On the condition that he would loan me a few books, I agreed to take a shot. I devoured a massive amount of information quickly, made an outline, thought up some examples and then faced the fifteen adults with heart-pounding apprehension. Getting through the first class was tough, but I was asked to return. People seemed to like my "I'm learning, too" style. After several months I was hooked. Two years later no one was more surprised than me when Father Knight invited me to direct the entire program.

The yearly RCIA experience crescendos and culminates during the liturgical seasons of Lent and Easter. On Holy Saturday, those seeking to convert experience the rites of initiation into the Roman Catholic faith. The rites are designed so that the whole community, not just the individual seeker, is plunged into a forty-day retreat (Lent) and is then immersed into the passion, death and resurrection of Christ (the paschal mystery). Year after year I spend great energy teaching Scripture and theology, planning the rites and executing an elaborate retreat based on these themes. The more I meditated on the events of the paschal mystery, the more I learned the lessons of the Marian story. In essence, the entire life of Jesus is the model for our own lives. Everything that happened to Jesus happens to all of us— birth, ordinary time, a public life of love, suffering, death, resurrection, ascension and Pentecost. Christ's life provides very clear instructions on how we are to live the greatest of all human endeavors, that is, how to truly love others with a gentle and nonviolent heart.

Most Christians have some theological understanding of the passion of Jesus. We know the events, we know the feelings and although the story often makes no rational sense to us, it nonetheless resonates deeply somewhere within the heart. The power of the story rings true to our own life experiences whenever we sacrifice for love. There is a honeymoon period followed by a move into a more intense relationship where love is on trial. We feel alone, as Jesus did, in the garden of Gethsemane, sweating blood over our commitment as we strive to go beyond feelings and sacrifice everything for the beloved. Facing the possibility of love's demise catapults us to a place of profound existential aloneness. As the cross finds all of us, we know we cannot escape death. We spend time in the darkness of the tomb. We rise again when we allow the light of a more mature love to pierce the darkness. And when we are able to let go of the past without resentment, we can ascend, like Jesus, so that a new Pentecost, a new spirit of love, can come and make its home in us.

Our lives embody a recycling of the birth-death-resurrection-ascension mystery whether we realize it or not. We do not choose to be born into the paschal mystery, but we do have an attitudinal choice about how we face its challenges. The popular question, "What Would Jesus Do?" (WWJD) begs a response from every love relationship in our lives. For if we apply the events of Christ's life to our own, the answer is simple: Persevering through pain, suffering and the many deaths we experience on a daily basis with gentleness of heart contains the greatest hope of new life.[5]

ELLEN'S STORY

I met my friend, Ellen, when we were both invited to be speakers at a women's morning retreat several years ago. As I sat and listened to her story of conversion and transformation, married to a Jewish man who had never really practiced his faith, I felt an immediate connection. As we got to know one another over the years, we talked extensively about our relationships. We were both amazed and affirmed by the realization that our lives in their small ways had been illuminated by meditating on the paschal mystery. Ellen's story was particularly striking. Although born into the Catholic faith, she drifted away, as I did, during college. Pursuing a career in the medical field, she eventually became a high-powered executive in healthcare advocacy. Ellen admitted to many past relationships, including a first marriage that failed. However, when the true love of her life came along, they married and have enjoyed twenty-eight years together. Since neither of them was practicing any religion when they met, no importance was placed on their diverse backgrounds. It was not until Ellen's mother became terminally ill that a spiritual awakening occurred and the course of their lives dramatically changed. With the help of friends, guides and her own dogged tenacity, Ellen began practicing Catholicism again.

Ellen confessed openly that her return to faith was the biggest challenge of their strong and committed marriage. "He couldn't get his little finger around it," was how she described it to me. However, she also believed fervently that if she just kept talking and he listened long enough, he would get it. There were dark moments when she thought they might even break up over the issue. While this terrified her, she was prepared to accept a failed marriage if there was not room for the Holy One to be present in the relationship.

Like me, Ellen started her spiritual odyssey by praying and going to church alone. After a series of remarkable experiences of divine presence, she summoned the courage to tell both her husband and grown daughter what was going on in her soul. "I thought maybe I was losing my mind for a while," she said. Since her husband is a psychiatrist, she asked him to evaluate her mental health. Relieved that he didn't think she was delusional, Ellen shared her growing fervor. His response shocked and blessed her: "God is calling you." Then they had numerous talks. Ellen told him everything. She said he listened patiently most of the time, although he was obviously nonplussed by this new turn of events in their long marriage. From time to time, he even vented his frustration: "How dare you bring this awesome force [God] into the middle of us?" Ellen said she didn't blame him for not understanding since her conversion was quite unexpected. She felt that some outside help carrying the growing tension between her love for God and her husband was needed. A trusted spiritual director who walked with her through the transition was enlisted.

Ironically, Ellen's breakthrough moments came when her consciousness was raised regarding the connection between the Jewish feast of Passover and her Christian experience of the Passion. She learned that the word *paschal* means "Passover" and this further piqued her interest. Ellen then carefully reread both the Hebrew and New Testament texts. Doors opened. One realization led to another. Soon she and her husband were having a conversation about his Jewish roots and the God of Israel. Ellen persistently pointed out that she thought her conversion and their marriage were inextricably bound together. She was thoroughly convinced that his Judaism had everything to do with her Christianity. A particularly illuminating day came when they went to see a priest together who confirmed Ellen's perceptions and invited her husband into a rich dialogue. Together they inspired each other. Ellen began to attend classes at the local temple with her husband. He agreed to have their marriage validated in the Catholic church. They began to observe Shabbat on Friday nights, and once in a while they went to Sunday Mass together. In the midst of such growth, Ellen said she gradually became aware of how profoundly the symbolism of the paschal mystery had affected them. Their relationship had suffered, died and was resurrected. Letting go of the past, they had both ascended to a radical new birth of love that continues to expand in its embracing vision.

SOME FINAL REFLECTIONS

Whether it was the gentle yielding of my husband to a four-foot-tall statue of Mary or a simple awakening to the sacredness of everyday life, I was pleased to no longer compartmentalize my spiritual journey. Ellen's story confirmed for me that a singular and sometimes lonely path could be a powerful force for change. Regardless of how awkward or unsure we are, regardless of whether or not we openly share every thought, word and deed, the divine presence gently begins to surface everywhere when we have eyes to see.

As with any love relationship, a rebirth of faith produces a whole new reality full of mystery and possibilities. Beginning with a honeymoon phase when eyes are wide open to wonder, we feel connected by a force that drives us into union. When the intensity recedes and life's demands increase, we experience, once again, our existential aloneness on the planet. Our restlessness may force us to feel like we have to move on, to find another mountaintop, another person, another religious experience to feed our insatiable hunger. While the desire is not wrong, maturity comes when we can find the ecstatic moments in the relationships we presently have, in the ordinary events of our everyday lives. We don't have to bounce from person to person, church to church, experience to experience to make God more fully present than right here and right now. We simply have to learn how to attune ourselves to the divine music constantly mediated through all relationships.

Meanwhile, God knocks gently on the doors of our hearts, reminding us that we are not alone. Each human encounter is potentially an experience of the divine, flowing freely and constantly through time. We live, we love, we suffer, are misunderstood, we die over and over as we take the risks required of intimacy. But when we enter fully into those deaths, like Christ, we experience continual resurrection. We are all invited to actively participate each and every time we say yes to love.

CHAPTER THREE

SOLITUDE
AND
COMMUNITY

My wrestling with loneliness described in the last chapter was greatly reduced for a while after the births of my second and third daughters, Elizabeth and Caitlin. My husband and I had almost given up all hope that we would ever have any other children despite medical information to the contrary. Nine years had passed since Aimee made us parents in our twenties. After many trials, we quietly accepted the possibility that she would be an only child. Meanwhile, we bought a business and moved to the beach community of Dana Point, and I finished graduate school. Just into my third year of college teaching, I found out I was expecting our second child, nothing short of a miracle in my mind.

Elizabeth's birth, even now after twenty-six years, still inspires in me a sense of great wonder. The Marian images of openness and receptivity became crystal clear to me during the pregnancy. While every child is a pure gift, Elizabeth's presence in my life was a constant symbol of God's sublime power. Three years and nine months later, we were thrilled to welcome our third daughter Caitlin, yet another affirmation that life was fecund with God's presence. Suddenly, our house was overflowing with toys, noise and baby contraptions. One day, tripping over blocks and stuffed animals on my way to the refrigerator for the juice Elizabeth demanded, I came face-to-face with the reality that I wasn't alone anymore. I was too busy teaching, dealing with Aimee's homework, the needs of a pre-schooler plus a little baby to feel anything but fatigue. As many mothers of small children do, I would escape from time to time into the bathroom just to be alone for a few minutes. Even then, one of the little ones would be banging on the door wondering where I was. Gone were the early morning prayer and journal times. Gone were the hours of listening to tapes and reading the spiritual classics. Many times, falling into bed at night exhausted, a fleeting thought that I hadn't prayed much that day filled me with lingering regret. While loneliness had indeed subsided, the need for solitude had increased threefold.

Yet another paradox had presented itself: the drive and command of Christianity to love others coupled with the growing need for solitude. When you are knee-deep in children, family and urban dwelling, balancing these seems highly unlikely. When you are walking through the spiritual journey without a mate's support, this monastic-like existence seems nearly impossible. How I would manage the demands of spiritual growth while simultaneously answering the call of marriage and motherhood loomed a monumental task. Yet, as much as I felt like giving up, I was also determined to find a way to reconcile the two opposites.

THE SPIRITUAL MEANING OF SOLITUDE

Solitude is a ubiquitous concept in spiritual literature. All the great saints and religious writers attest to its necessity if one is ever to "advance" in the spiritual life. They talk about the benefits of extended silent retreats and hours devoted to contemplation. To be honest, I dismissed most of these writings, especially the ones written by celibates and medieval scholars. Instead, I searched, mostly in vain, for married saints struggling with spouses who did not understand the spiritual journey. However, when I began to read literature by modern contemplatives, I found some interesting insights that changed how I viewed solitude to a much healthier way.

James Finley, a former student of Thomas Merton, talks in detail in his many books on contemplative prayer about the innate solitariness of life. Evidenced by the fact that whenever we draw upon life's hidden resources, the need to be alone increases. Just as great artists, writers and scholars crave such solitude, so do those who journey inward in search of God. The opposite of isolation, which makes us feel anxiously alone, solitude leads us to subsist in a profound unseen unity with all of creation. In that sense, Finley says, solitude is a relational term referring to the quality of our interior awareness which gives meaning and purpose to our outer lives. In essence, he says that solitude is determined by God alone, who, creating us in image and likeness, calls us into relationship. We stand alone in God's presence as the beloved, just as we do in marriage. "You and only you are the one I love. Only you in all of creation can fulfill my desires for fulfillment in love by accepting my love and loving me in return."[1] What an insight! While the notions stirred and burned inside, I needed to put "some skin" on this deep theological reality. As before, I looked for role models and found them in the most unlikely places.

MONKS, TAPES AND PRAYER

The monks, both men and women, of the Spiritual Life Institute provided the basic guidance and depth of understanding that I needed. I never dreamed that hermit monks would have anything relevant to say to an urban-dwelling woman married to a spiritual outsider like me. However, when I met several of them at the Los Angeles Religious Education Congress in the early 1980s, I was immediately captivated.[2] How alive they seemed, joking and laughing easily, listening like I was the only one in the room. I was enchanted with the women's long hair pulled back by a small kerchief and the light brown robes they wore. Most of all, I was intrigued with their definition of a mystic as someone who knows God by experience.[3] Insisting that mysticism is as natural as breathing and imbued in ordinary life, they debunked my slightly spooky, esoteric misunderstanding. "Do you know God by experience?" they asked me directly. "Well...um...sure...I mean I think so," was my stammering answer. "Then you are a mystic," they pronounced with delight. At first I found their quick statement ludicrous. No one felt more stumbling on the road to spirituality than I did at that moment. Then the monks challenged me to become even more mystical, that is, to expand my experiences of God by living life "to the hilt." This sounded enticing and exciting but what did they mean, exactly?

Desiring to know more, I subscribed to their publication *Desert Call* and sent away for their monthly tapes.[4] I listened while I cleaned my house and walked the babies in their strollers. Whether it was the headphones I wore or just my own voracious need to connect with God in the flesh, I felt the influence of their words imprint on my brain and sink deep into my soul. I slowly began to understand Christian humanism, a thoroughly natural approach to life abundant. The joy that exuded from their invitation to "take a long, loving look at the real," was intoxicating.[5] As I gazed one day with my girls at an intricate spider web built across our pathway, I was flooded with the sense of wonder. The presence of the Holy One was palpable as we appreciated the Creator's handiwork. The solitude that came from walking alone on the journey had given me a new vision. I might not have consciously chosen the solitary path in marriage but I began to understand that there really is no other way. The spiritual journey is a singular journey shared with others whenever life presents the simple gifts we stop and appreciate.

I was also inspired by the monks to write my own rule of life. They had spent years formulating and living what they intended to do with the time God had given them. Impressed by their vision of "disciplined wildness," I wanted to participate in the full and abundant life promised by Jesus.[6] I wanted this life for myself but I wanted it even more for my family, believing that this was the greatest gift I could give them.

So, with the resolution of a monk, I sat down and made a plan for my spiritual life, something I thought I could reasonably stick to. While I wanted to have hours of contemplative prayer each day, I knew I was setting myself up for failure. I had to begin on a smaller scale. So I scheduled in fifteen minutes in the morning and fifteen minutes at night. That was all. Since my husband was an early riser, it wasn't that hard to get up at least thirty minutes before my children. We made a pact not to talk for the first half-hour, much easier for him (an introvert by nature) than for me (the wild extrovert who likes to comment on everything). He would start the coffee and pour me a cup. After a few sips and a glance at the newspaper, I would then go to my designated prayer chair—a blue Adirondack outside on my back patio in the summer, an antique blue wingback right beside my fireplace in the cooler months. Sometimes I would light a candle but always I would set a timer. With eyes closed, I would simply breathe in a little prayer and settle down into silence. I asked for nothing and tried not to engage in whatever thoughts were brewing. After the fifteen minutes, I wrote down any image or word that seemed significant. Then I intentionally carried those symbols in my soul throughout the day, noticing if they "fit" anywhere else.

This simple fifteen-minute discipline was the beginning of many more periods of intentional solitude and became the basis for living a contemplative life amid the chaos of work, motherhood, marriage and service. At night right before bed, I would repeat the ritual. Since I was the only one awake, the greatest difficulty was turning off the television and fighting an inclination to go to sleep. I finished the fifteen minutes by asking God to speak to me in my dreams. Often, I would remember nothing. Some other very special times, powerful symbols arose.

A DREAM OF LIGHT

One such dream came to me about a year into my fifteen-minute meditations. Walking alone in a meadow filled with waist-high grass, I looked up at the sky and saw dark, ominous clouds gathering overhead. I searched frantically for shelter but finding none, I knelt down in the grass as three bolts of lightning struck. The first one hit a distance away, the next one came closer and finally the last one hit me, lifting my body off the ground. The heat of it was palpable. I smelled charred earth and skin. Then the rain came and formed a pillow of water that buoyed me up toward the heavens. As the storm subsided, a beautiful rainbow stretching from one end of the horizon to the other appeared. Everything in the meadow was illuminated with golden light. When I returned to the earth, I was walking down a crowded street. I felt an urge to reach out and touch the other people and when I did so, an electric shock went through my hands into the sagging shoulders of the passersby.

I awoke then with a pounding heart. The dream seemed so real that I had to get up and look outside to see if everything was bathed in light. My disorientation abated when I looked at the clock and saw it was 4:00 AM. I remained awake for another hour and wrote the details of the dream in my journal. In the subsequent months, I reflected on the dream many times. A growing sense of mission, based on the interior solitude I had begun to cultivate, began to emerge.

That no one accompanied me in the dream seemed especially significant. I walked alone, content in my solitude until the clouds overhead made me afraid. How so like my journey just then. I loved my solitude but feared the potential storms it might bring into my life. When I surrendered to the rain, my fear diminished with the beauty of an inner baptism of light. I decided maybe I was being told to stop worrying about whether or not my partner was with me on the path and start trusting that I would be given the energy I needed to grow on my own. Maybe the trinity of electricity that surrounded and pierced me, that is, the illuminated earth (the first strike), the illuminated path (the second strike) and the illuminated individual (the third strike) meant that spiritual power is available to everyone. Maybe, and this was the most crucial truth of all, when we are called into solitude we are given the power to create meaningful relationships. The consequence of intentional solitude with God, then, cannot be divisive. Rather, the generated energy creates the bonds that hold people together.

Admittedly, dreams like that are few and far between but the ramifications are not. Months later, while I was facilitating a retreat, I shared the dream reflections with the group. Consequently, people were moved to share their own experiences borne out of solitude. An amazing number of individuals talked about dreams full of storms and lightning bolts. The discussion went on for more than two hours and was the impetus for many persons to intentionally reflect upon the potential messages received from ordinary experiences.

Later a very special gift was given to me from my friend Pegge who had continued to carry these dream images in her consciousness. In a dusty corner of her favorite thrift store, she found a poster-sized photograph of a storm with three bolts of lightning striking the earth. We laughed together at the serendipity of this find and she helped me hang the poster in my tiny office. For years afterward, I would gaze at it and remember the connections between the inner journey of solitude and the radiant light meant for the life of the world.

SOLITUDE, MARRIAGE AND COMMUNITY

As the children grew and more wedding anniversaries went by, the need for solitude continued to increase but so too had our understanding of that need. I had established foundational priorities. Both Dana and the girls by then were used to my silent sits, the journal writing and the long walks I took with our dogs. We talked openly about timing, such as when it was appropriate to ask about daily activities, homework and having friends over. The delicate balance of integrating contemplative life into a very active, loud and bustling household was oftentimes stretched to the limits. There were days when I felt all was hopeless and other days when the light streamed in so naturally I felt just minutes away from heaven.

Back and forth, up and down, in and out like the waves at the beach, I thought one summer day as I watched the girls boogie-boarding in the surf—that was me and my attempts to find solitude, to grow in the spiritual life. Without anyone to talk to about this endless tension, I was driven toward books, books and more books. I remember reading the book *Mystical Passion* by Father William McNamara on the beaches of Maui during one summer vacation.[7] Completely absorbed, I was startled into reality when a stranger on a towel nearby asked what I was reading so intensely. Glancing down, I saw that she was reading the latest Danielle Steel novel, making me all the more self-conscious. Rather offhandedly, I said I was reading a book about spirituality. That led to a short, awkward exchange of one-liners that made me realize how intensely private and protective I had become of my interior musings. I had absolutely no desire to talk to her—or to anyone, really—about my spiritual life.

What was up with me? I wondered as I later made a paper covering for my book in an effort to conceal its identity and avoid further intrusions. Had walking alone in marriage made me a spiritual recluse? Had I held my spiritual life too privately? Had I become a rugged individualist with a "Jesus and me for all eternity" mentality? Certainly it was worth consideration. Thoughts came over me that I could not stop. Maybe I needed to invite others into this solitude and intentionally engage them in talk about spirituality. I felt both resistance and an energy urging me forward. What would happen if I did reveal my life in community? How would that affect my relationship? Once again, I turned to books on the contemplative life and back to the beloved monks of the Spiritual Life Institute for wisdom and insight.

It turns out that the monks had a lot to say about the benefits of community. While they lived solitary lives in their hermitages during the week, they came together each Sunday for worship, communal meals and fellowship. Their relationships were enhanced by their intentional solitude and rule of silence for six days of the week. They were very big on celebrating the Sabbath in community. The lively discussions and laughter they shared with one another heightened the anticipation of companionship. The intentional communication they practiced produced a deep intimacy among them. In the midst of this reading, I played with the thought that, in an odd way, I was sort of living the dual solitude and community life the monks described being married to someone with whom I could not discuss the spiritual life. I saw myself as a hermit while at home, retreating to an interior solitude that was intensely private. On any given day, I could go to community for liturgical prayer and camaraderie. Perhaps I could have the best of both worlds if I just gave community a chance. True, the kids were always banging on the door of the bathroom but they could not intrude into the deep interior life I was developing and neither could my husband unless I allowed the interruption. Intentional solitude and meaningful community was up to me and turned into a greater challenge than I ever imagined.

The awakening moment on the beach, though it made me realize how privatized my faith had become, also brought to consciousness the possibility that I had no language for spiritual experience. Since I didn't really talk to anyone about interiority, feeble attempts sounded so childlike and trivial. The need to find others who might share my passion grew as did my disquiet. My relationship with God was grounded in experience at that point, without spoken words. Puzzlingly complicated, communication about the divine presence often overwhelmed me into the silence I was used to in my home. Incredulity also went along with this self awareness. Wasn't I the one with a master's degree in public speaking and communication skills? Wasn't I the one who debated any issue, could wax eloquently on a variety of topics at the drop of a hat and was poised and confident in college classrooms? True enough. Yet, here I was, tongue-tied and anxious, metaphorically on my knees, like Zechariah before the Great Mystery. This reality became all too clear when I was invited to substitute teach in a junior high religious education class. My knee-jerk reaction to this request was an immediate no, but I quickly changed my mind, deciding that my talk about God was probably best tested on junior high students who might not be listening that closely. I felt like a miserable failure after the first attempt only to be asked back again and again. I recall thinking after each weekly session that they had to be desperate to want me. Limping along like the walking wounded, I was humbled by the insights of these young people who talked so freely about God and the Spirit. When the year ended, I was so grateful to them for helping me find my spiritual voice, weak and stammering as it was then. They had also provided me with a sense of community, a place to connect where other adult dialogue might be possible.

PITFALLS OF WALKING ALONE IN COMMUNITY

Those of us who walk the spiritual journey alone in marriage are susceptible to a great many pitfalls, some from our own self-doubt and some from the judgments and misunderstanding of other people.

Through my volunteer work with youth, I began to establish personal relationships. I could now name people I used to only recognize in church on Sunday. I became a familiar face in the crowd, teaching religion once a week, attending daily Mass with my two youngest daughters at my side. Always alone or with children in tow, I did not feel so different attending church during the week. I saw many others without partners. Later I found out that many wondered about me. My friend Jerry fondly remembers seeing me at daily Mass and wondering about "that single mom with those two cute girls." Another remark I heard repeatedly after introductions was "Oh, you *are* married. I thought you were divorced." Others would chime in that they didn't want to pry but speculated about my life. Single? Married? A widow? I fought the urge to ask them how they explained the babies that kept appearing. But I did not, realizing early on that such remarks were rarely intended to hurt me. I philosophized that their assumptions about my singular presence were just a reality one had to accept. However, like a never-ending backache, I carried the pain of feeling branded as I forged my way alone in a faith community that held traditional Catholic marriages and family as the highest ideal. Many people remain unaware that such an attitude perpetuates a subtle discrimination against the one walking alone in faith, creating a barrier that is not easily overcome.

A somewhat disturbing reality exists in parish schools that give preference to children whose parents are both Catholic. For many years, due to limited space in the elementary school, each family seeking entrance into the system went through a series of interviews. During that time, I received many calls from families turned down because one of the parents was not a practicing Catholic. Thinking that I had some inside influence, they would ask me to plead their case before the principal. Despite my best persuasive attempts, I was usually unsuccessful. There had to be some way to "weed out" the many applicants, I was told. Intact, committed Catholic parents seemed only a fair and reasonable standard. Not realizing the anguish of the Catholic parent walking alone in faith, decisions made without malice nonetheless ripple across multiple levels. As one woman said after being turned away from the school because her non-Catholic husband would not come with her to the interview, "It felt like the last judgment." Getting over her own disappointment was further complicated by explaining the rejection to her cynical husband. Any hope of changing his mind about church was dashed to the ground in that one decision. Such unfortunate endings are not deliberate and not uncommon. Wonderful, well-meaning people uphold the ideal Catholic marriage for noble reasons that should not be totally disregarded. However, Sunday morning Mass attendance is evidence that women either there alone or with children far outnumber traditional families. Like any marginalized group, they often suffer silently due to lack of awareness and sensitivity. Truly, the time is ripe for changing attitudes.

Another case in point happened during the first few years after my return to the church. By this time, I was working in parish youth ministry and surrounded by dedicated volunteers also interested in the spiritual journey. Although no one shared my situation (married to a nonparticipant), they nonetheless were willing to discuss books, ideas and inner struggles. Many of them wanted to talk about their Cursillo experience, a retreat designed to invigorate and renew the active faith life of both individuals and parishes.[8] I listened with rapt attention as they talked about the life-changing experiences they had on this Thursday through Sunday overnight event at the diocesan center. Their riveting testimonies made me inquire about going and I had many enthusiastic offers of sponsorship. However, I soon learned that there was a catch. If you were married, your spouse had to go too. In fact, men went on the first weekend, women on the second. Not realizing the extent of this problem for me, friends assumed that my husband would be interested or at least just acquiesce and go for my sake, as many other spouses had done. They were certain that if they could just convince him to go, he would have a conversion experience and our lives would dramatically change.

In my mind, asking Dana to go to Cursillo was like asking him to jump off the Golden Gate Bridge. I knew it in the depths of my being that there was no way he would agree, and I dreaded even asking him. After praying about it for several months, I finally put my hesitation aside and broached the subject. Sure enough, he said no. I didn't cry, scream, protest or even gently coerce. I just accepted. I did feel grief over a lost opportunity, over what seemed like an opening door. Because he would not go, I could not go, that was the program's rule. Some of my friends even petitioned the movement to allow an exception for me, but it was never granted. One by one, the majority of my friends and colleagues went to Cursillo and continued to "group" (get together for weekly faith sharing sessions). As they did, I felt more and more left out and alone on my singular journey within community. (Thankfully, Cursillo has since relaxed this rule.)

The prospect of going on a different type of retreat was continually before me as offers came in here and there. Despite my negative experience with Cursillo, the idea of going on a retreat remained appealing to me. After another stab at possibly going to Marriage Encounter (he wasn't interested), couples' retreats were ruled out. Consequently, I began to think and pray about the possibility of going alone and how I could manage the obstacles I faced. A long weekend spent on a spiritual retreat is often a very difficult thing to explain to a partner who is not in the least bit religious. I also had serious questions about what would happen to me and how further interior changes might affect the relationship. I was afraid that growing closer to God might increase the distance between us. And so I put it off and promised myself and God that someday in the far, unspecified future, when the kids were not so needy, and my husband was ready for it, an opportunity would arise. The admonition to "be careful what you pray for" became real to me in a very big way when that opportunity did come knocking soon afterward. (More on this in chapter six.) Through these and through the experiences of others in the same predicament, I was struck by how the insidious constraints of walking alone in community threatened to roadblock the ever-widening path into God.

FINDING SUPPORT IN THE COMMUNITY

Even though I felt alone, I knew I was not. There were many others in the community like me. We just did not know each other because nobody was talking. I decided then and there to begin sharing my story every chance I got, hoping to spark some interest and most of all, to raise consciousness about this important pastoral concern. Eventually, after many years of working in parish ministry, I founded a support group and began working directly with others in the same situation. Interestingly, though many people I talked to individually agreed it would be a good thing to do, not many actually came to the meetings. Those who did, however, bonded and remained together for several years. Sharing our stories, we became a small circle of friends who knew that someone else understood. Most of all, we learned that a strong and committed marriage with Christ at the center could happen for us, albeit in a different way. Solitude could become our greatest source of strength instead of our greatest obstacle.

SOME FINAL THOUGHTS

Walking alone in a faith community without a spouse has its own set of blessings and problems. Naming and facing those realities is the first step in accepting, rather than fighting, what is inevitable and perhaps unchangeable. Many well-intentioned people, trying to be supportive and positive, often tell me to just "pray about it," invoking the seventeen years that Saint Monica prayed for her son, Saint Augustine, to convert. While I do not rule out "giving it to God" in prayer, my experience has always been the same. Namely, that sometimes when I give it to God, God gives it right back to me. Prayer doesn't work quite the same way we wish it would. Ultimately, I only have myself to work on. I can only change my own set of expectations, my own attitudes. Solitude and contemplative prayer, when I sit with my hands and heart open and listen rather than directing and begging God to do what I want seems the only sane and spiritually fulfilling way to go. Such a stance teaches me to be at peace with my situation, to rest in God's loving presence to transform and heal, to remain a humble servant instead of a dictating steward as I walk alone in faith.

PART TWO

WALKING
TOGETHER

If you are not comfortable with paradox, you will never be comfortable with Christianity. Father Richard Rohr, a Franciscan priest, author and sought-after speaker, taught me that valuable lesson many years ago.[1] Observation of the human condition and the laws of nature confirm this nebulous reality. The first half of this book has focused on the singular nature of spiritual journey. Whether we are married or not, no one may accompany us as we plumb the depths of our interior lives. How we live with the consequences of growth and stagnation, longing and loneliness, solitude and community forms our spiritual orientation.

Simultaneously, the spiritual journey is about walking together. While we are alone on an interior landscape searching for God, the exterior of life brims with others who both lead us to and distract us from the divine. We are born from and for relationships. The future of the human race depends on that fact. While we can avoid intimacy and the deeper realms of self-revelation, we cannot and most of us do not want to escape making a human connection. Pathological behavior often results from the inability to bond with others. The human heart naturally reaches out with dogged persistence and resilience. We want someone to walk with us through the human adventure and the quest for God is no different. Faith communities are testimony to these desires. Throughout history and multicultural experiences, people have banded together in their worship of the Holy One.

I grew up in a small Minnesota town that had a church on every corner. Surprisingly, three of them were Catholic churches in a town of barely fifteen thousand people. The Midwest is no exception though. Everywhere you look when you travel the world, tangible evidence of the need to connect on the spiritual realm is there. Temples, mosques, churches and campus ministry centers dot the landscape with symbolic clarity. We want to and do walk together in faith. No wonder that at some point those of us on the serious spiritual journey yearn to share the experience. The relationships that we establish and maintain, from casual friends to intimate lovers, have a great deal to teach us not only about ourselves but also about God who formed us in the divine image and likeness.

CHAPTER FOUR

Mystery
and
Relationships

As a young girl in a Catholic school, I remember always having my hand up when one tough doctrine or another was ambiguously explained. After exasperated attempts to answer my many questions, I was often silenced by "it's a mystery." I translated that to mean don't even ask, there are subjects beyond comprehension. Never quite satisfied, I spent my early life trying to solve the inscrutable. God and relationships, my two favorite subjects throughout graduate school and well into the second half of life, were always the final common denominators in the search for truth. Now I have utmost respect for "the mystery," beginning with the tantalizing taste of freshly brewed morning coffee to the rapturous smell of night-blooming jasmine. Mystery makes life a wild and passionate adventure, one I bow down before every day. Mystery has become the home where I dwell barefoot with God on sacred ground.

Observance of couples walking around on this earth teaches a valuable truism: Relationships seem very mysterious. How did he get with her? How did she end up with him? How do they make it work? Or don't they? Perhaps most mysterious of all are long-term relationships of forty or more years. Sometimes the two look like they do not even like each other, let alone possess a love strong enough to endure time's travails. We dismiss past eras of our parents and grand-parents as markedly different times, way before the openness of modern relationships. Few couples divorced then, certainly fewer Catholic couples. Some experts point out dysfunctional family patterns or the lack of opportunities for women as the explanation. Regardless, like the Trinity, the Incarnation and a host of other religious concepts, relationships often remain mysteriously inexplicable.

That said, I will now make a seemingly contradictory statement. Relationships, in all their mystery, are also very predictable. Having been married thirty-eight years, with twenty-something years studying and teaching interpersonal communication, I say that with confidence. One has only to look at the developmental nature of relationships to fully understand this paradoxical reality.

THE DEVELOPMENTAL STAGES OF RELATIONSHIPS

Posing the simple question of how couples met, I hear predictable responses. Friends introduced them at parties or they met in college or at work. Some disliked each other instantly, others fell in love immediately across a crowded room. Different as the stories are, all started out with minimal personal information about each other. Even couples who grew up together in a similar environment talk about not considering the other as a potential partner until some enigmatic moment when a different form of communication began and a shift in feelings took place. This progression of stranger to intimate partner is usually not all that mysterious.

The early stages of relationships are marked with ambiguity and the exchange of impersonal, safe information like comments on the weather. Communication with strangers on the street follows a predictable pattern based on cultural norms that are learned by imitation. These patterns vary somewhat across cultures and yet are remarkably similar. We don't speak to people we do not know unless it is out of necessity—the store clerk, the person we bump into by accident and so on. We make little eye contact; we do not stand close. We remain silent in elevators.

What makes a human encounter move from stranger to acquaintance is also quite predictable. The variables of time, frequency of interaction and socially acceptable information are stepped up. In several encounters either in the neighborhood, at work or in social situations, I find out your name, where you are from, relatively "safe" bits of information like the kind of car you drive, what restaurants you enjoy or the last movie you saw. When the encounters are pleasurable experiences, the two often find themselves looking forward to seeing one another again and begin to increase the frequency of interaction. Dating carries the possibility of transforming the acquaintance to what they might both call "friend," the next level of development.

Just as before, time, frequency of interaction and the type of information exchanged deepens the relationship. Discussions at the friendship level are now beyond culturally and socially acceptable topics. Information becomes personal and when reciprocal, intensifies over time. I tell you about the problems I'm having with my family, what I worry about in the darkness of night, my future dreams. Then you reciprocate with the personal drama of your life. That nebulous dynamic, trust, begins to cement the relationship as attraction and care grows. Each person feels honored to be the keeper of secrets and esteemed to be known as a special confidante. Willing to sacrifice precious time and self-centered tendencies for the sake of the other, the friendship becomes a priority.

Relationships expand from friend to intimate by more meaningful sharing, even more time, and yet another defining ingredient, exclusivity. Now the other person is the only one who knows my deepest feelings, thoughts and experiences. The mutual willingness to share on this level convinces the couple that this relationship might be "the one" and the question of marriage naturally arises. Such intimacy, the kind that makes couples want to stay together, takes a great deal of time and effort to cultivate. All other relationships fade into the background for a while. Our human capacity to manage and maintain such intimacy is limited. Yet another dynamic, physical intimacy, separates this specific relationship from all others. When one feels known, loved and cherished so deeply, eros, a driving force, captivates and intoxicates the couple. The insatiable nature of the human spirit marches toward union with alarming passion. When the feelings of love are exchanged and are at the highest peak, the desire to meld into one another can sometimes ensnare the couple into a relationship without boundaries. The marriage vow, "forsaking all others" becomes an experienced reality.

Many times I hear young couples boast that they have given themselves totally to their partners, disdainful of friends who do not understand. A certain look of pride accompanies the statement. They conclude that these friends are just envious of their "joined at the hip" appearance and are not real friends at all. Mistaking the togetherness phase with authentic intimacy that develops slowly over time, such a relationship may become an idol for a while, worshiped and adored at all costs. If this happens, interest in God often greatly diminishes. The object of love becomes the only god they desire to know.

Eventually of course, the fervor of the early stages wanes. Practical needs, if nothing else, move us back to the surface quickly as other people, work and menial tasks interfere with the moments of union. As time goes on, an interesting phenomenon occurs. We discover that no matter how satisfying the relationship remains over time, the human condition cries out for more. The realization that no single relationship completely satisfies us may come as such a disappointment that we question our decision to love in the first place. Some think that the marriage has been a horrible mistake and divorce, only to repeat the cycle again. Sadly, many people chase the heightened feelings of the early days of intensity all their lives. While they know this is a myth, the driving need for union sometimes overwhelms rational understanding.

Others stay in relationships anyway, accepting the inevitable changes that come as the challenges of growth and daily life occur. Commitment to the relationship, despite the hardships and confusing feelings, slowly brings about a ripened and mature intimacy that allows for interdependence. The continual yearning to unite with love remains simmering underground as the decision to remain in the relationship, no matter what, solidifies.

The maintenance of an intimate relationship remains an important challenge as the years go by. Backsliding into the impersonal communication that dominates most of life easily happens. Awareness of the developmental nature of relationships coupled with commitment to intentional acts of love help to keep the levels of intimacy high. Acceptance that communication continues to evolve into simpler forms must be faced. Fewer words are spoken. More time is spent comfortably enjoying silence, as when couples can sit for long periods of time simply holding hands without saying or doing anything. This more contemplative phase spreads itself like a comforter over the marriage as children grow up, grandchildren are born and the frenzy of the early stages of the relationship move to the horizon.[1]

A MIRROR OF THE DIVINE

The study of relationships completely occupied my thought process while I was writing my master's thesis so long ago. Fascinated, I began to see the drama of the stages played out in every couple I observed. Long about this time, friends were divorcing, others just getting together. Meanwhile, I was already in my tenth year of marriage. The cycle of stranger-acquaintance-friend-intimate was like looking at a long river moving predictably over doldrums, rapids, weather changes and stagnancy. I could see the blueprint everywhere, and I felt as though the lights had come up on a bright new configuration.

Painfully, I analyzed the patterns of my own ten-year marriage and came to the rather startling realization that we had married during the acquaintance stage of the relationship! My husband proposed to me just weeks after meeting me in Greece despite my protestations that we didn't know each other well enough. Promising to visit me in Minnesota when he was discharged from the Army in several months, we began a torrid love affair through letter writing. Today it seems rather quaint to think about that, but writing to someone every single day forges a different type of quasi-intimate communication. I found myself telling him things I would never have had the courage to say in person. Swept away in the romanticism of it all, we nonetheless got to know sides of each other that would have undoubtedly remained hidden in normal circumstances. We wrote about love, marriage, attitudes toward politics, money, sexuality, children, goals and dreams for the future. It is no wonder that when we finally did get together, we felt like close friends, maybe even intimates, even though we had now only known one another for a total of about six months. So young and with so much idealism and sweet naïveté, we married, blissfully thinking we had enough information to sustain us.

Obviously, despite the revelations of the letter writing, there were a great many things that we did not know about each other. Living together as married partners was something altogether different from the romantic ramblings of young people in love. We had many awkward moments, many adjustments to our personal likes and dislikes. He didn't know how much I loved to read, especially at night in bed, and I didn't know how much time he wanted to spend playing golf. I didn't know the full extent of the pain he had suffered because of his parents' divorce, and he didn't know how much my Catholic upbringing had formed my feminine dependency. We had hidden, as most couples do, the shadow sides of ourselves. However, since we had spent so little time together, these concealed areas were mostly untapped. We spent the first few married years learning how to be friends amidst many misunderstandings, squabbles, fears and tears. What kept us together? Now it is my turn to shrug and call it a mystery. Maybe it was our early written pact never to divorce or give up on one another. But maybe not. I cannot say for sure. I can only say that the moments of real intimacy emerged very slowly, like hidden bulbs that break the surface of the cold earth here and there, scattering their colorful essence on an otherwise nondescript landscape.

Looking back to that tenth year when my study of relationships made the pieces of the big mosaic of my life fit together, I felt both unsettled and hopeful. For some time, regrets plagued me as I awakened to the reality that achieving intimacy was a slow process that we had tried to achieve hastily. Conversely, I was comforted to know that intimacy could wax and wane over many years without necessarily causing a breakup. Finally, as I sank down deep into commitment with my husband, only to again feel the restless yearnings for something more, I accepted the fact that this was how it was going to be, not just with him but with everyone.

Unknowingly, that acceptance set the stage for the spiritual awakening that was lying dormant underneath the drama of my marriage. I slowly began to see that I did not need to move on to another man, another relationship, another time and place to explore the ongoing hunger for intimacy. Instead, the time had arrived to explore this relational dimension with God. Mysteriously, walking together in marriage had brought me to this new threshold of being and to the realization that I was on the brink of a life-giving, albeit life-changing, encounter.

Very soon after this stark but ultimately good illumination, I began my sojourn back to my home in Catholicism. Despite constant inner resistance, the mysterious pull of a new relationship with God was undeniable. My heart leapt when I recognized the familiar pattern of relational development. For many years, God had remained a stranger to me because there was no intimacy between us. Our communication was typically impersonal and infrequent. When I did go to visit God at church, the exchange was perfunctory, based on cultural and social norms. I began with the Sign of the Cross, recited the parts of the Mass without any cognition, left the church behind and did not think about God anywhere else. Communication theory taught me what had to happen if I wanted a deeper relationship with God. I had to let the conversation between us progress to another level and more often. Sure enough, when I began to talk to God on a daily basis about the details of my jumbled life, a new friendship developed. Reading, praying, listening and writing eventually moved us from friendship to the same intimacy I had desired and experienced in marriage. The mysterious longing for complete and total union with the Holy Other increased over time. I finally understood by experience that the outer search was over. I had found the ultimate love relationship I so desired.

The knowledge that the marital relationship is, in essence, just a mirror of the divine relationship constantly fills me with wonder and delight. When we fall in love with God, choose intentionally to communicate personally and frequently, and are committed for life, creative union happens. Perhaps that state could be defined as "heaven," the deliberate practice of becoming one with God for eternity. Not a reward or even a goal we achieve from living a virtuous life, arriving at such bliss may be the natural consequence of simply saying yes to intimacy each day.

THE MYSTICAL MARRIAGE

The mystics who talk about God as lover and bridegroom are evidence of this powerful reality. Called the "spiritual marriage" or "spousal love," such a relationship is characterized by the language of lovers. The biblical Song of Songs or the spiritual poetry of Saint

John of the Cross and Saint Teresa of Avila are just a few of the many examples found in spiritual literature.[2] Contemplative or mystical prayer, like a silent love letter, is full of passion and desire for the ecstatic union of opposites. As one becomes more familiar, more intimate with God, communication predictably becomes intensely personal and unique to the relationship. Eventually, there are no more words. The chatter over the trivial goes away, replaced by the beautiful silence of the mature married couple, content to hold hands and gaze into the sunset together. These readings helped me understand the importance and attraction of contemplative prayer. God's arms are wide open and always inviting, but the choice to fly into the embrace is mine alone. Just as so many people balk at the commitment, the nakedness, the transparency of allowing another to know their darkest secrets, I balked at the immensity. The enormity of God was overwhelming but there was no turning back now. Once again, that slippery eel of a concept, trust, came back to reassure and whisper "just let go into the mystery."

Over the years I have collected a plethora of stories from individuals who have answered the call into intimacy with God. They all talk about trust. They all talk about a kind of darkness, a type of dryness, a fear of surrendering the will. Often the relationship at this stage feels like an affair accompanied by guilt, secrecy and temptation to run. Some feel as though they need to curtail the spiritual encounters, others feel they need to separate from their spouses and enter monasteries. Human desires are often paradoxical, setting up black-and-white categories and "either/or" choices. We want it all, true, but we do not know how to handle it all. Thus, the tendency to destroy one path when we choose another is strong, especially when it comes to love. As we have seen, we are also limited in the maintenance of truly intimate relationships. However, in relating to God, the resemblance to human encounters ends. While human relationships are finite, the God relationship is infinite. The bonding monogamy of deep marital love is but an extension of the eternal *agape*, the unconditional love of God. That is, the more I learn to love you, the more I learn to love God. The more I love God, the more I learn to love you. That's just the way it works.

Revelation: My relationship with my nonparticipant husband (or anyone else I love) does not have to diminish my relationship with God! These two intimate, simultaneous relationships (one human, one divine) actually constitute the plan of salvation. The vertical intimacy one experiences with God intersects with the horizontal intimacy one encounters in others. We have the capacity to sustain both. The transcendent nature of God's love (unlike our human capacities), draws and embraces all of creation. Thus, my deep, intentional and intimate relationship with God is meant to enhance all of my other connections. I get a taste of the divine in the intimate human moments of deep committed love.

ANNIE'S STORY

Living out these lofty connections provides reflective food for those of us who walk spiritually alone in marriage. Annie's story is a perfect example. Annie and her husband, John, a self-proclaimed agnostic, had been married about fifteen years when she chose to attend my annual women's retreat. Around the circle, I asked participants to say why they were there. Annie laughed and said it was simply "to get away from the kids for a weekend and to be with other women on the beach." Immediately during the first session, I recognized a familiar look on her face signaling to me that transformation was happening in Annie's soul. As I watched her throughout the weekend, she became quieter, wrote a great deal in her journal and strolled alone on the beach during every break. She shared very little during the group discussions but wept copiously over everyone's stories. Saturday night, when all the women were going off to bed, Annie asked me for a private talk.

We sat in side-by-side beach chairs on the patio, delighting in the smell of the ocean and the full moon's gleam over the waves. I listened intently as Annie confessed her secret love life with God and how John had so ridiculed her beliefs at the beginning of their marriage that she had hidden any outer appearances of spirituality. "Even when I took the children to church, I would act passively because I didn't want them to tell Daddy that Mommy was crying after Communion," she related. When John called Jesus "her boyfriend" and said he could never measure up, her inner pain intensified. No one, not even her closest spiritual friends, knew the extent of Annie's love for God and her subsequent anguish over hiding it. Holding onto what Annie called, "a slender slip of hope," she wondered how she and John could ever stay together when they were so different. Then suddenly, a crisis happened. Annie was diagnosed with breast cancer. Through surgery, radiation and chemotherapy, John's abiding love and devotion toward her was an incredible comfort and source of healing. Annie's voice quavered as she talked about her experience of waking up in the recovery room after a radical mastectomy. She thought at first that she was looking directly into the face of Jesus, divine light pouring into her soul. Never had she felt so tightly held in the embrace of unconditional love. However, as Annie became more conscious, she was startled to realize that it was actually John's face she was seeing.

In those moments of suspended time, Annie believed that God had allowed her to peek into a piece of the great mystery of relationships, namely, that there was really only one source of love. John's love and God's love were the same. There was no separation. Despite their opposite positions, Annie realized on the retreat that she had learned more about the spiritual journey from her marriage to John than anywhere else. With her cancer now in remission, Annie said that her feelings of sadness and anxiety over walking alone in faith had also taken a turn. John still was not participating outwardly in her spiritual journey. Yet, somehow, he was at the center of it.

THE DEEP-DOWN KNOWING

Several years ago, during a Guided Imagery with Music retreat,[3] I found a name for the experience that Annie so poignantly spoke about. This retreat is a process of spiritual direction that uses classical music and imaginative meditation to foster a deeper relationship with God. During the sessions, a guide helps the participant to remember the images that come from the musical meditation. During the silent hours alone between the sessions, the individual works with the images to uncover what God might be trying to communicate. I had no expectations going into this retreat. It had been a busy year and I was looking forward to eight days of silence and solitude. If nothing else, the idea that I could just rest was appealing. Truth be told, I was in the midst of a five-year desert experience in which my prayer was dry and God rather distant. Years on the journey had taught me to accept the situation with resilience and detachment.

No one was more surprised than I was when the sessions were brimming with symbols, emotion and light. There were so many images that my guide could not write them down quickly enough. With classical music as the background, the movie of a spiritual marriage played out, scene by scene. There was a celebratory sense, a party going on inside my soul and it was all about Jesus, my husband, my family, my friends and how they were all a part of a larger, universal love that God has for the planet. Without going into detail, those eight days were like a week of constant lovemaking. I experienced what I have come to call "the deep-down knowing."

In essence, God is teaching us in the depths of contemplative prayer, in everyday ordinary situations, and especially through every relationship, that there is really only one love story. Everyone and everything is about that story. What we do with the people and circumstances in our lives is up to us but when we stop and really look, we see that all of it points to the God relationship. Everyone and everything brings us back to this deep-down knowing, knowing that union with God is the ultimate destination. We may have to sweat blood in the garden for love, as Jesus did at Gethsemane, and we may have to bounce back from the many conflicts we experience on the Via Dolorosa of our lives. However, in the end, we can only ask, as Peter did when Jesus wanted to know if he was going to leave him, "[T]o whom shall we go? You have the words of eternal life"(John 6:68). That was Peter's deep-down knowing, the same as for all of us.

MYSTERY YET AGAIN

The mystery at the heart of every intimate relationship brings one into the realm of a new understanding. As I ascend into intimacy with God, the people I allow close travel with me. That is the created order. As I stand at the nexus of the cross such intimacy creates, I fall more deeply in love with all that is revealed through both encounters. This beautiful and rather simple realization poses its own set of problems and dilemmas. Achieving this kind of intimacy is not by any means easy. Pouring oneself out to another person and to God takes discipline and tenacity. As one person in spiritual direction wailed, "Intimacy is such hard work!" Then, after pausing for tears and sighs added, "But so worth it!"

The imprint of the divine on all human relationships remains a constant source of growth if we have the courage to see. Whether we share the same path of faith or not, the opportunity to come into full communion with God springs from all encounters. Learning to read the symbolic language of intimacy helps us to embrace the deep mystery of all relationships—why we are here together right now.

CHAPTER FIVE

CHILDREN
AND
FAMILY

Along with my personal fears about embracing a spiritual path, a host of issues arose about how this decision would affect the family. When the journey began so many years ago, my oldest daughter, Aimee, was only eight years old. Embracing the faith was easy for her. She willingly and sweetly went to church, was eager to take religious education classes, and adapted naturally to her mom's changing patterns of behavior. Once in a while, Aimee would question why her daddy never went with us but rarely did she challenge him or me on the subject. It wasn't until Elizabeth and Caitlin came along that I had to sort things out once again.

As an old truism goes, when one person in a family gets a cold, another person sneezes. In essence, decisions within families affect everyone, not just the person making the decisions. The spiritual journey of one person is no exception to this rule, especially when children are involved. When only one parent desires to practice, there are many questions to consider. What happens when the nonparticipant spouse is in opposition to raising the children in the faith? How much does tacit agreement and noninvolvement affect the faith life of the children? Does indifference have a negative outcome? How do I explain the noninvolvement in a positive way? What should I do regarding the religious education of the children? How far should I go in "spiritualizing" the home? This chapter will attempt to answer these questions and give some practical suggestions for creating a more harmonious home.

WHAT CHILDREN SAY

Because I have contact with many children and youth in our religious education programs, I have been able to pose the question of nonparticipation directly to them. Most children under the age of ten seem unfazed as to whether or not both parents go to church and most report that Mom is the one who takes them. Where is Dad? Without any judgment, they say he had to work, mow the lawn and other assorted answers. As children move into the preteen and adolescent years, a change in attitude often occurs. Many become sullen about practicing the faith and begin to recoil at the very activities they seemed to enjoy as youngsters. Anxious parents express their incredulity about what happened, thinking that the discord is somehow their fault. Psychology has proven that just as some kids breeze through adolescence easily, a great many others stumble and bumble, making life miserable for everyone else in the family. When it comes to practicing the faith, even the ones who seem well adjusted in other areas sometimes become quite obstinate and spiteful.

When polled, the teens in nonparticipant families frequently question why they have to go to church when Dad (or Mom) does not. Since adolescence is a natural time when abstract thinking is kicked up to a much higher level, this turn of events is predictable. Since beliefs in Santa Claus and the Easter Bunny have long been uncovered as myths, in the same manner, beliefs in God, Mary and the saints are held up for scrutiny. Some teens exhibit uncertainty, others indifference and still others downright rejection of what they had no trouble accepting in the past. With only one parent in the household participating in matters of faith, the challenges of dealing with such turmoil can be overwhelming. Many times the exasperated parent gives up and allows the rancorous teen to stop practicing the faith.

Every year when I interview adults seeking the sacraments of initiation (baptism, confirmation and Eucharist), the stories come full circle. Those who grew up in nonparticipant situations most often report feelings of confusion, sadness or even anger regarding the spiritual ambivalence of their parents. Poignantly, one young man told me that even though he had strong inclinations toward religion and loved going to church, he sublimated his desires because he worshiped his dad and didn't want him to think he was being disloyal. "I acted like I didn't care one way or another about believing in God." Another middle-aged woman told me that she and her mother had to lie about where they were going when they went to church because her father was so adamantly opposed. "He said he didn't care if Mom went but he wanted me to be free to make up my mind when I became an adult." Eventually, her mother grew weary of fighting the losing battle, especially when her daughter lost interest. They gradually just stopped going to church and never spoke about the subject again. "I got the message that religion was not as important as keeping peace in the family."

While some adults express sympathetic understanding of situations they did not quite understand as youth, most of them do not want to repeat the cycle. Interestingly, the adults who return to the faith of their childhood often do so to establish solidarity with a

practicing spouse. Many view religious division between parents neg-
atively and do not wish to bring their own children up in such an
environment. They hope that coming back to the church will bond
the family and change the dynamic. (I am happy to report that this is
often the case!) Meanwhile, many other adults, reflecting on their
unconventional upbringing in the faith, say that they admired the
parent who had to persevere and take the children alone to church. In
the words of a son, "My mom's faith was so strong that when she
prayed, I believed she had an inside line to God." In the words of a
daughter, "I thought my dad walked on water because he took us to
church by himself." Conversely, there are others who say they admired
the parent who did not participate. "He wasn't a hypocrite," they say
admiringly. "She acted more loving than most of the people I knew
going to church all the time." Rare is the individual who says living in
a family divided on faith is preferred. Many adults express feelings of
sadness for the one who did not participate. "I felt bad for him, on
what he was missing." "I worried about her salvation." "I adamantly
rejected the faith because I couldn't believe in a God who would con-
demn someone as wonderful as my father." "I fantasized what it
would be like in a family like my friend's, who seemed so happy and
united at church."

The faith life of children is affected, both positively and nega-
tively, by the nonparticipation of a parent. As with many aspects of
life, the outcome can go either way and there are no predictions or
guarantees. Obviously, a great deal depends on a host of other
influences besides how the parents choose to express their spirituality. Perhaps the most common problem faced by the participant

parent is how far to go with imposing religious beliefs on the children when there is no support at home.

TO FORCE OR NOT TO FORCE

When young parents call the church and request baptism for their newborn infants, most parishes require them to attend at least one class before the sacrament takes place. During this session, among other things, they are told that baptism is the entrance into the Christian life, one that should span a whole lifetime. Godparents are informed of their duty to oversee the religious upbringing of the children in case the parents fail in this mission. Most of the time, all of this information is dutifully accepted and there is a sense of hope in the decision to rear the baby in the faith. Thankfully, this statement of intention and the ritual that subsequently happens in community constitutes a wonderful experience for those involved. I suppose one could call the first step of initiation "forcing" the baby, but most see it as a response to God's invitation, a good thing for everyone.

As the baby grows from preschool to elementary age, the sacramental life of the community continues to embrace and form these little ones. At about age seven or eight, the second part of their initiation into Christian life happens as they receive the sacrament of the Eucharist for the first time. A sense of celebration accompanies this event and when done within Sunday liturgy, first Communion is a hopeful witness to future generations. Not long after the grace of such an event, many children begin to express some resistance to the routine of church and religious education classes. Parents often ask me what to do when this happens. While it is a common occurrence regardless of whether or not both parents practice, the decision to "force" religion on children can be very perplexing. The frustrations of harried parents often result in these rationalizations:

> "Religion is a very personal thing, so maybe I shouldn't impose my beliefs."

> "I am afraid I am going to completely turn her off by my insistence."

> "Since he hates going, he can choose for himself when he's an adult."

> "She says they don't do anything in confirmation class, it's a waste of time."

> "I am embarrassed when my children are disrespectful and won't participate at Mass."

The list goes on and on. My advice is always the same: Be strong! After raising three daughters, I know how hard it can be. Consider replacing the word "force" with "discipline." Just as we discipline our children to eat right, get enough sleep, work and play hard, we also need to offer them the discipline of faith formation. Just as they resisted toilet training, brushing their teeth and eating their vegetables, they will resist the discipline of learning and practicing the faith. But that does not mean you should give up trying. Choose your battles but make faith a priority instead of a casualty.

Children need a foundation in the faith. They will not be able to decide for themselves later if they have no information on which to base an intelligent decision. The Christian faith, especially the Catholic faith, is a very adult proposition. With a long and checkered history, the doctrines are dauntingly complex. The paschal mystery, at the heart of our faith, does not begin to make sense until the second half of life. (Paradoxically, by that time, many have ceased to practice.) Meanwhile, there are children to be reared in this faith. We simplify religious concepts, explain theology at their level of development and tell Bible stories like they literally happened. We take children to Mass week after week and they learn by osmosis what to do and say. So often they do not learn what religious practices have to do with their personal lives. For a variety of reasons, many adult Catholics do not know how to talk to children about the complexities of our historical church nor are they comfortable verbalizing spiritual experiences. Why? Because many adults do not realize that they are caught in a repeating cycle of stunted faith development and what they need to do to break it.

THE REPEATING CYCLE

Children are enrolled either in religious education classes after school or they go to a Catholic school. They study a very complicated faith in classes adapted for specific age levels for roughly ten years. In tenth grade (in some areas eighth or ninth) they receive the sacrament of confirmation. Teens are told that they are now considered fully initiated adults in the church. With a sigh of relief, both students and parents think they are done with formal religious training. For the rest of their lives, they sit in the pews with a ninth or tenth grade education about God and the faith. Quality and quantity of what they know all depends on the rigor of formal religious education, competence of religion teachers and reinforcement at home.

Small wonder why many adults feel empty, disconnected and inadequate as they sit at Mass each week, struggling to maintain the challenges of adulthood with a childlike or adolescent faith. It is not surprising that others leave looking for meaning elsewhere. On balance, those who stay and seek out a deeper understanding of faith are richly rewarded for their efforts. Many have a profound experience they say they never knew existed before. In essence, the journey of faith that begins with an experience of God in childhood, and is reinforced throughout elementary and high school, is ultimately meant to be a lifelong adventure. Unfortunately, a disconnection often happens between the religious experience of adolescence and the gritty realities of adulthood. A vast number of adults are unaware of the second half of life's adventure into God that can sustain them through old age.

SPIRITUAL CONNECTIONS

When I do spiritual direction, I usually begin by asking my directees to recall their earliest experience of God. The majority talk about going to church with a parent or grandparent, learning their prayers, rituals such as baptism and First Communion. When I point out that they are talking mainly about religious experiences and encourage them to think "outside the box" about *spiritual* experiences, the stories become much more inclusive. Many talk about childhood wonder at the beach, feeling overwhelmed by the immense beauty of the mountains, experiencing the love of a parent. Connecting these experiences with religion then forges a new pathway, one that makes sense out of the rules and rituals that may seem meaningless. Without such connections, the seeker is at a loss to describe what is going on inside, doesn't know what to do with innate longings for the God experience. In the words of Richard Rohr, we need a "container for faith first" before we can decide for ourselves to discard it.[1]

When my two youngest daughters were about seven and eleven, the older one began to complain about going to church. "Do we have to go?" she implored week after week. My rather cryptic-sounding answer was always the same: "No, we don't *have* to go, Elizabeth; we *want* to go." Every time I said it to her and she rolled her eyes at me, I knew that she could not possibly understand at such a young age what I meant. Nonetheless, I had to try to communicate something very important about the spiritual journey that I hoped would make sense to her later on into adulthood. We move beyond the Sunday obligation when we fall in love with God. When this happens, we want to spend time in worship. In changing just that one word, I hoped to change the way my children thought about our practice. The reaction came sooner than expected from the mouth of my youngest, Caitlin. She would get herself dressed on Sunday mornings and say to me, "When do we want to go to church today, Mommy?"

Teaching our children about the divine encounter is not always easy, especially when they resist. However, when certain activities, such as going to church on Sunday or attending religious education classes are not a choice left up to the feelings of a child but rather are intentional decisions of committed adults, children usually accept the routine as unchangeable. Growing up, my three daughters knew that Sunday morning meant Mass followed by a trip to the local donut shop for breakfast with friends. Now adults, they fondly remember those days. For the most part, all three enjoyed studying religion, and we had many interesting discussions about God, the church and morality. Whether children resist or respond, providing the container for the faith most certainly has a positive effect in the long term.

Most professional religious educators today are comprised of married laypersons with children. We were trained in the basic premise that parents are the first teachers of their children.[2] Since the earliest images of God are most often parental, children cannot grow into adult images without moving through stages of faith development tied to these experiences. Realizing that you and God are synonymous for a while makes an important case for conscious, early formation. While there are no guarantees that children will continue to believe or practice the faith, parents only have the moments of early childhood to shape what kind of thinking will come later. I believe it is best to take advantage of these years when the heart opens easily to hearing the story and there is no trouble believing in an all-loving God.

PRAYER AND RITUALS AT HOME

Two families united for a potluck Thanksgiving dinner one year. The holiday table held a beautiful spread of fall colors, china, silver and even place cards hand-decorated by the children. The familiar aroma of roasted turkey with all the trimmings naturally drew everyone to the meal, abundant with delicious side dishes and specially baked pies for dessert. Since it was Thanksgiving, the mother of the family announced to everyone that they should say grace. "GRACE!" shouted the dad, making the children and other adults laugh. When the giggling subsided, an awkward silence and then an argument over who would actually say the prayer of thanks ensued. Finally, the perturbed mother quickly did a rote recitation that not everyone knew. As the bowls were passed and the noise level grew, the mother sat quietly in her chair pushing down the urge to cry. Her vision of the perfect family meal was shattered because she did not know how to benignly lead her family into a simple prayer before meals. Frustrated and embarrassed, she was confused about imposing her need to pray onto the whole group.

Carting the children off to church or religious education classes is usually quite doable for any parent walking alone in the faith. However, discord often arises when one tries to incorporate prayer and any other religious rituals in a home with only one participating parent. I know that last story well because it happened to me a long time ago when I was still new at walking the spiritual journey alone. While your circumstances will dictate what the course of action should specifically be, I have three suggestions that might help to pave the way.

1. *Make grace a sharing ritual.* When in the situation of Thanksgiving or other large gatherings with the whole family, I make grace into a special time when the family talks to each other. A special blessing cup filled with any beverage is placed in the center of the table before the family gathers. Instead of just saying a rote prayer, I ask everyone to name a blessing for which they are grateful. The cup is passed around the table and each person takes a sip after he or she has shared. This can also be done with a loaf of bread or by passing a single rose or a lighted candle. The act of passing and speaking gets everyone involved in sharing the often unvoiced blessings and concerns of the family. When every person at the table has had a chance to speak (and some even to cry), discussion at the meal often takes on a whole new tone. No longer does grace have to be a fast and awkward mumbling—rather, the cries of the heart are unloosed and everyone feels heard.

2. *Pray at bedtime.* Rituals at bedtime have long been lauded as an important part of getting children to sleep through the

night. Brushing teeth, saying good night to everyone, a drink of water and the obligatory bedtime story all help bring a comforting order to the end of the day. But nothing helps a child slip into a peaceful place in the dark like bedtime prayer. Whether you choose to kneel down or whether you snuggle up together, the bedtime prayer can be a combination of rote and spontaneous prayers. Children can be taught the Guardian Angel prayer easily with its rhyming cadence. They can be taught to "God bless" the people they are most concerned about. If done consistently, you will be touched by how many people (and animals) the children include. One mother told me that her son prayed every night for the endangered whales. Another told me that her daughter was most concerned with African children sick with AIDS. Many children want to pray for ailing grandparents or friends missing from school that day. Many feel compelled to pray for the parent who does not practice. The feelings of powerlessness that children often feel in our fast-paced world often get assuaged as they pray in the hushed moments before sleep. Such prayer provides a way of sharing the intimate communication that usually just goes on in private. Most of all, praying together establishes a habit that invites the child into a personal relationship with God that, as we have discussed, ultimately mirrors the human experience.

3. *Teach contemplative prayer.* Like ducks to water, children take to silent contemplative prayer with ease. Even the extroverts seem to appreciate a chance to be quiet for a while. The use

of instrumental music may create the pathway into the experience of silent prayer. Beginning with a simple prayer such as "Speak, God, we are listening," and ending with just "Amen" works well.

The contemplative method teaches a child that prayer can be done anytime and anywhere. No vocalized prayer is imposed on anyone else. Children often become reluctant to express themselves when they have to endure the awkwardness of praying in front of nonparticipant parents. Silent prayer allows everyone privacy, an intimate moment before God not formed or manipulated by words.

Perhaps it seems like I am advocating a watered-down version of prayer when I talk about teaching modalities that are kept private and quiet. Obviously, there are times when children take the lead with open acts of piety along the way. As I have stated before, you have to find the method that works best for you and your family. However, in most instances less is better when sharing public expressions. In the words of one young adult, "Nothing turned me off more than when Mom made us pray in front of Dad."

TALKING ABOUT GOD AT HOME

A saying attributed to Saint Francis advises us to preach the gospel always, using words only if necessary. If I am translating Brother Francis' philosophy correctly, he means that we convert more people by our actions than by our words, a thought that rings true. Since I teach theology and am a spiritual director, I talk about God a lot. Although I feel fortunate to have this luxury, I often fear that spirituality and religion just as easily remain lofty ideals if one is not diligent. In the homes of us walking alone in faith, here is the chance to really see if we can put into action what we say we believe.

When my children were growing up I did not quote Scripture to them constantly, did not talk about God at the dinner table and did not drill them on faith essentials *unless they asked.* I let them set the agenda and allowed talk about the divine to emerge naturally in conversation. Did that ever happen? Yes, more times than I could count. The magical moments of childhood are full of God experiences that children have no problem verbalizing. The questioning times of young adulthood lead to serious theological discussions over setting the table or folding the laundry. Making sense out of the suffering and deaths children inevitably experience as they grow can provide multiple opportunities to talk about God at home. The gradual unfolding of the mystery during these discussions happened many times in front of my husband. Since nothing was ever staged, I tried hard to use words that were natural and explanations that were not preachy. Treading delicately in a household divided on faith is hard work, no doubt about it. However, the alternative turns everyone off, frequently splintering the household even further. Most importantly, the need to talk about the nonparticipation of a parent must not be ignored, glossed over, or commented on with distain. Why doesn't Dad (or Mom) believe? Why doesn't he go to church with us? Will he go to heaven? These are common questions that children may or may not verbalize. Again, wait until asked to broach the subject and most of the time, give simple answers:

> Why doesn't Dad believe?
> *I don't know why, but I know that God loves him anyway.*

Why doesn't Mom go to church with us?
She isn't Catholic, or she doesn't practice religion, so she
doesn't feel the need to go.

Will he go to heaven?
Of course! He is a very good person. God knows his
heart, so we don't have to worry about that.

When children grow into adulthood, the discussions about why Dad or Mom never practiced will become more complex, of course. Always communicate to your children, who love the nonparticipant parent, that God is a loving and just God. Don't let them worry about salvation, grace or what they heard happens to nonbelievers. Take the burden off children so they do not blame themselves for discord in the family.

OF STATUES, CROSSES AND OTHER RELIGIOUS SYMBOLS

Cindy, a young mom with three children, married to Chris, a non-participant, stopped me outside of church one day to tell me that she had just purchased two three-foot oil paintings of the Sacred Heart and the Immaculate Heart of Mary at an antique store. Enthusiasm about the "good deal" she had wrangled was mixed with foreboding. Engulfed in more than just "buyer's remorse," she did not know how to tell Chris that she wanted to hang them prominently in their living room. "I want to consecrate our whole home, and I don't care who knows." Cindy's face looked faintly like Joan of Arc to me, her jaw set and geared for battle. Cautioning her to go slowly, I invited her to come and talk a while before she hung the paintings. Sadly, she did not. I heard some months later that Cindy and Chris had split up because, in the words of friends, she had become "too fanatical" about her religion. While I am sure the breakup was more complex than simply hanging religious pictures, there is something to be learned here.

As I previously related in chapter two, I had my first encounter with religious objects in the home when my oldest daughter yearned to host the traveling statue of Our Lady of Fatima. Once over the initial hurdle of resistance, I slowly began to put up religious symbols here and there. I put tiny crosses in each of the girls' bedrooms. I decorated my fireplace with primitive angel art. I discreetly tucked statues of Saint Francis and the Madonna in the outside flower beds. In doing so, the inner sanctuary that was burning brightly with many imaginary icons gradually materialized. When I allowed myself to find, use and display sacred objects, a nonverbal opportunity to communicate my feelings about the spiritual life appeared. While Dana never objected, another friend reported that her husband complained loudly that she was turning their house into a shrine. That's when she moved her big statue of Mary into the spare bedroom. Discretion is obviously very important!

Each person walking alone in the faith must find a comfort zone here. I certainly advise discussing with your spouse a purchase like large oil paintings prior to laying down any cash. Respecting the space created together as a family is sacred in and of itself. Otherwise, decorating with religious articles that are only meaningful to one person can be seen as a violation, a kind of trespassing on personal choice. I do have another suggestion that may help bridge the gap.

CREATING A SACRED SPACE

Creating a sacred space on a table in a corner of the home provides a reminder of the divine connection that is unobtrusive and easily assembled. Cover any small table with a beautiful cloth, purchase a large scented candle and place it in the center. Add things that are natural and symbolic of God's presence such as rocks, shells, fall leaves, feathers, fresh or dried flowers. You might add photographs of grandparents who live far away, newspaper clippings that have touched your heart, mementos of trips or special occasions. A friend of mine has a map of the world displayed on the wall behind her sacred space, symbolic of her commitment to pray for peace. Objects may vary as the seasons of life change. The list of what may end up on the table is not limited. Anything that serves as a quiet, intentional statement of the spiritual life may be included. The sacred space then becomes a way to teach children, family and friends how to interpret the ordinary as a continual, intimate message from the Holy One.

The spiritual objects you decide to place in your home, whether they are blatant works of art or natural items disguised with meaning may spark a reaction from the nonparticipant spouse. But maybe not. It is important to be prepared for either one and not have any expectations. In the midst of slowly decorating our home with spiritual articles, my husband seemed quite unaffected. We rarely discussed my choices, and he never protested. While I was grateful for his lack of resistance, I was also a little disappointed that he never seemed to notice what to me was a radical shift in consciousness. I silently wondered if he knew the real me at all. Then, one Christmas, something changed.

TWO GIFTS

That Christmas (also my birthday by the way), my husband was very excited to present two special gifts he had chosen himself just for me. Since this was uncharacteristic of his gifting pattern, I opened each one with a little apprehension. Much to my surprise, the first box contained an authentic Russian icon of Jesus. He explained with great delight that a golfing buddy's wife imported sacred images from world trips and that he was able to purchase this one from her. The second box contained an unusual set of Russian matrushka nestling figures. Seven hand carved images of the Madonna, patriarchs and prophets from the Old Testament fit inside each other with delicate precision. The story of Christianity unfolds from the first twelve-inch figure of Mary holding the Christ child down to the tiniest two-inch patriarch.

I could not find words that day to express what was and is still deep within my heart. Somehow my husband had chosen the perfect gifts for me. He had reached beyond his own needs, crawled into my intimate and sacred space before God and had chosen something off the shelf of my inner sanctuary. His love for me had made him keenly observant of what was being transformed right before his eyes in our home. This signal of transcendence was a reminder to me of the invisible and silent power of God. Beginning then, I created an icon wall in our living room that is still in process today. Other sacred pictures center on the Russian icon of Jesus, the gift that continually affirms the spiritual journey of walking alone and walking together in faith.

CHAPTER SIX

FRIENDS
AND
GUIDES

Many couples I know refer to spouses as "best friends." As one man said, "we are not only in love but are also in like with each other." I could tell that he was right as I watched them interact at various church functions. They were always completing each other's sentences, reading the same books, going on fabulous vacations together. Despite twinges of envy, I tried to simply accept the fact that I might never experience such compatibility with my spouse. Yet as I grew to know and love my dear friends Mel and Jo, I learned that in addition to the togetherness of forty plus years, they still needed other companions to make life complete. "Even though we share the faith, we are on two different paths when it comes to God," Jo confided the day she asked me to be her spiritual director. While they have many friends, she was not able to speak openly to anyone, even Mel, about her intimate relationship with God. "I can't keep this to myself any longer—I need you!" she cried.

Walking together means not only walking with family and children but also includes friends and guides sent to teach further lessons about the divine relationship. When you are walking the faith journey alone in marriage, the need is even more intense. Finding and maintaining these spiritual friendships has its own set of challenges but is, at the same time, a healthy and necessary endeavor. This chapter focuses on some of the more salient issues, including how to find a spiritual companion, the role of self-disclosure, the retreat process and, finally, the need for spiritual direction.

O BROTHER, WHERE ART THOU?

Spiritual friends don't just drop out of the sky but I have to say, in my case, the first encounters I had happened by accident. While I was in graduate school, I became friends with three wonderful women also in the department: Shirlee, a Southern Baptist, Lydia, a faithful Catholic, and Rita, an evangelical Christian. Even though I had known them as undergraduates, we never talked much about God or religion. One December, we decided to get together socially, vowing *not* to discuss the department, our seminars or anything remotely academic. We gathered as a circle of friends to engage in an activity as far from our graduate studies as possible—to craft a Christmas wreath for the upcoming holidays.

The conversation drifted over many subjects that night, but eventually, the topic of religion arose. Soon each of my friends gave testimony about their spiritual paths. Astonished but not showing it, I listened as they spoke about inner conversion, prayer and commitment to God. Since I was still haltingly unsure about my faith, I said very little. I felt like I was the questioner in the classroom again. We talked about God for so long that we actually spent the night. Fighting back tears many times, I wondered why I felt so emotional. At the end of the evening, Rita sensed that something was stirring and asked if I wanted to pray. At a loss for words, I just nodded and then wept as she prayed with fervor for God to forever touch our hearts. She and I stayed awake for yet another hour. Rita said she was certain that God was calling me to something great and all I needed to do was listen.

That first encounter with spiritual friends was a turning point for me. The next morning as I drove on the southbound freeway toward home, I decided to stop at the beach for a few moments of solitude. I remember looking out at the predictable waves pounding on the surf and feeling a new sense of gratitude. If God was calling me into relationship as Rita declared, at least I knew there would be companions that I respected. And even though my spiritual journey was but a small ember then, the message was clear that if I decided to let the fire burn in me, I would have the support I lacked at home.

Today, reflecting on that encounter some thirty years later, I feel overwhelmed as I think about all of the people God has sent into my life. Admittedly, they didn't just randomly knock on my door and find me. I made some deliberate choices that put me in a direct collision course with others who were seeking. After formally joining a parish, I began by volunteering (albeit reluctantly) to teach religious education classes. Difficult as that was, I met many wonderful men and women who opened their arms and invited me to go to seminars, retreats and classes about spirituality with them. The closeness we developed was like nothing I had ever experienced. We became friends on a whole different level I never knew existed. Questions were being answered as new ones appeared. Growth was happening. The silent chasm that existed between my husband and me on the topic of spirituality was filled with the rich perspectives of many different individuals. Everyone wove a golden thread through the beautiful tapestry of life.

Faith communities provide many opportunities to find and nurture spiritual friends. Most churches have myriad support groups, adult faith formation classes and volunteer positions. I always tell adults that the most difficult part is just going through the door of the event. In my experience, even the tiniest opening to the interior yields great results. If you want companions on the spiritual journey, you simply have to go where they gather and be willing to share your intentions. Don't wait for a personal invitation. Enticements are found everywhere these days, from parish Web sites to advertisements in magazines. Find something that sounds interesting and then make yourself take the first step.

SUPPORT GROUPS

A great way to connect with others also on the spiritual journey is to join or perhaps even form a support group. Support groups do just what the name suggests, namely, they provide a shoulder to lean upon. Like-minded people come together for the sole purpose of sharing their spiritual joys and sorrows. By committing to monthly meetings over an extended period of time (sometimes indefinitely), the members get to know one another's stories and be present to the ongoing journey.

When I searched for others who shared my unique experience of being married to a nonparticipant, I found many who commiserated. But while people expressed interest in talking about the subject, very few actually came to the group that I began. Fortunately, a few committed individuals can become a very meaningful unit. The group I met with over a three-year period consisted of four very different women who were open to sharing their challenges and suggestions. We listened with our hearts and souls to one another. We laughed uproariously together and many times we passed around the tissues to dry our sorrowful eyes.

Judy talked positively about her long marriage to a spouse who openly expressed his disdain for what he called her "childhood Catholic brainwashing." Paula shared her struggles explaining to both her spouse and children the importance of her conversion to Catholicism and her growing devotion to Mary. Eva's husband was not in the least bit threatened by her spiritual walk, but she did not know how to talk to him about God. We learned by listening to one another each month, and as we prayed together for all of our needs, the collective experience was powerfully healing and bonding.

The best way to start a support group is to begin sharing your plight with others. Notice individuals who always seem to be alone at church. Acquaint yourself with the organizer of the adult faith formation programs in your parish. Tell her or him about this book and your need to share with others in the same situation. Ask your pastor to consider allowing you to use the parish database to find others. Once established, brainstorm and set the agenda for the discussion to follow, including where and what time to meet. The group can then direct itself.

RETREATS

When my youngest daughter, Caitlin, was just shy of turning two and I was working part-time in youth ministry, the pastor of our church asked me to collaborate with an energetic, newly assigned associate to begin an elaborate retreat process for our teens. I believed that this was a sign from God. Personal circumstances had so far prevented me from going on a retreat. Now professional requirements would pave the way. I was excited that my job in youth ministry required that I not only attend but that I also learn the specific details of creating a meaningful retreat experience. Finally, a breakthrough had come in explaining the retreat desire to my husband: "Honey, I *have* to go," I said demurely. "It's part of my job." Small wonder I was met with little resistance beyond the usual inconveniences of finding round-the-clock supervision and fun activities to keep the girls occupied and happy. Best of all, these retreats were held at our parish facility. I didn't even have to travel far for the experience. Yes, most adamantly, I knew this was a sign.

From inception, the retreat process resonated with my soul in a way I would never have believed possible. It brought out and utilized the many gifts I had for creativity in areas of art, music, drama and public speaking. It fulfilled my need to verbalize what I had learned from the many hours of solitude and reading. Most of all, the retreat experience fulfilled my need for community in a big way. I actively searched out and established relationships with the many people who became part of the large teams I needed to pull off the events. They became my soul companions on the journey as we prayed, laughed, wept and reached out to the many youth, young adults and adults who flocked to the literally hundreds of retreats we provided over the next twenty years.

Probably more than any other part of my ministry, I became identified in our community as the person who led others on retreat. My children were constantly exposed to the fruits of this mission and I believe were greatly enriched by the growing community who now were like family members. I began holding retreat meetings at our home, inviting team members and their children to all of our family functions, talking outwardly, many times with my husband present, about God and the many wonders of our experiences. Gradually over time, my husband also came to know and love the spiritual friends who accompanied me on the retreat journey. He was blessed and gifted with people who accepted his individuality, people whose love for God was expansive, non-questioning and supportive.

The importance of carving out a weekend each year for a retreat became my most earnest soapbox, one I still stand on today. I realize more than anyone else how problematic this can be when your spouse does not share or understand. The obstacles on the path can seem like jumping hurdles every five steps. Nonetheless, I remain adamant in my advice to just do it! The roadblocks are in everyone's path, not just ours. We all can find a million plausible reasons to prevent us from going inward, our fear of the unknown clearly at the essence of our hesitation. But, as the saying goes, the only way out of fear is through it. Try volunteering to work on a teen confirmation retreat if you are not ready for the big leap of private introspection. The youth minister will be thrilled. At some point in time, I can guarantee that you will be casually reading the parish bulletin and suddenly an advertisement for a retreat will catch your eye. I challenge you to remember reading these words and see the ad as a beckoning from God. If you never push aside your fear and trepidation, you can ambush yourself from ever moving deeper into the divine relationship. After all is said and done, you will not regret going on retreat but you will regret the lost opportunity. The retreat will surely enrich your spiritual life and enhance your relationships, even with loved ones who may never understand.

SELF-DISCLOSURE: TO TELL OR NOT TO TELL?

While nothing is more compelling than entrusting someone else with what is at the depth of one's heart, self-disclosure may also cause great apprehension when the subject is God, religion and spirituality. Concern naturally increases for the married person who is afraid that revealing too much will be a breach in confidentiality. Questions arise: Dare I do this? What will happen if I do? Will my spouse resent me if I talk about our relationship? Ambivalence may block discussion of anything personal and while some resistance is normal, if left unchecked, it can become paralyzing. Guilt feelings can arise after disclosing too much personal information that feels like an invasion of privacy. As one woman put it, "I felt like I was betraying my spouse every time I talked about our relationship." At times like these, it is important to allow the inner voice to be heard. "You need someone to listen to you and with you." However, to quell the anxiety of who, how and when, a few communication guidelines are helpful.

First, focus the conversation on yourself, not the other person. Restructure your sentences by use of the pronoun "I" instead of "you," or "me" instead of "he" or "she." For example, you might say, "I feel lonely when I attend church every Sunday without my spouse." Rather than: "My spouse makes me feel so lonely when he refuses to go to church with me." This small change shifts responsibility for negative feelings back to the speaker. The decision to share personal information about your specific walk of faith thus limits the subject matter to your own interior musings rather than to inferences about anyone else. An acceptance of reality rather than playing the blame game will help keep the conversation from feeling too negative or derisive.

Second, establish boundaries around certain subject areas that are deeply intimate. Do not think that you have to take an "anything goes" attitude. There are some places in the heart that no one except you and God should be allowed to go. There are also some intimacies between married couples that should never be revealed to others. Spend some time in reflection and prayer over these boundaries. Realize that they are different for everyone. Reverence for individual disparities is perhaps the most important boundary of all.

Third, respect that there are appropriate times and places to reveal personal information. Timing is everything! Despite the urge to share something personal during a public setting, have the wisdom to count to ten first. If you are compelled to speak, rephrase, use general terms and do not use names without permission. Nothing is more devastating to a relationship than the awkward moments following a disclosure that is inappropriate. When in question, always ask permission to share something told in confidence before repeating it.

Fourth, respect the confidentiality of the person who has disclosed. There are moments in all of our lives when others reveal very intimate feelings and experiences. Some individuals openly request confidentiality while others are so immersed in the telling that they do not verbalize this need. Either way, self-disclosure of circumstances not widely known by others should be considered sacred ground. The importance of guarding your tongue against what can easily become gossip is tantamount.

Fifth, try hard to guard against projection. A projection happens when we take an interior feeling, like anger, and then make a judgment about the unstated motives of another person. For example, I am angry with my boss for challenging the goals of my department at a staff meeting. Later I say, "He did that on purpose to make me look bad in front of my colleagues" (Projection # 1). "He does not like me and he never did" (Projection # 2). I hear projections all over the place when I listen to people talk about their spiritual lives:

> "My children have all left Catholicism and are now evangelical Christians. The church failed them."
>
> "My wife does not believe the institutional church is necessary. She is just a product of the sixties and the feminist movement."
>
> "My husband is a good person, but he says religion is a crutch. He was born in Europe and they think differently than Americans."

Everyone projects. Let's just say human nature possesses the need to make sense out of life even when we are wrong. Become aware of your speech patterns. Take back the projections whenever you realize them. Refrain from drawing a conclusion that might be completely off base, especially when you are disclosing personal information to other people who in turn will repeat that projection when they talk to others.

Self-disclosure regarding one's faith remains a very personal dilemma, especially for those who cannot share the details of their spiritual journey with a spouse. Finding just the right support group may be difficult and then learning how much to share and how much to hold back can also be tricky. When these challenges present themselves as obstacles, the time may be ripe to consider spiritual direction.

SPIRITUAL DIRECTION

Despite great press lately about spiritual direction, I find that most people do not know what it is. Simply, spiritual direction is about intentionally inviting someone who has been trained to walk with you, to companion you, on the inner journey. Sometimes it is easier to understand what spiritual direction is not—it is not therapy, not pastoral counseling, is not about problem-solving. During spiritual direction, an experienced person is asked to listen to God's voice as you describe the ordinary events of your life. Spiritual directors do not tell you what to do or give advice. They mentor and guide. They suggest and affirm. They help you put words to the unspoken feelings and thoughts that come from the spiritual encounter. They help you answer the big question: "Where is God in all of this?"

The art of spiritual direction holds great promise for those who answer God's call to the deeper inner journey. Based on both my own experiences and the data collected from many others in the same situation, the need for spiritual companionship is great. The feelings of isolation and longing as one navigates through community life, raising children, service and stewardship are frequently experienced as threatening both to faith and to the marriage relationship. In spiritual direction, these feelings are not only explored but also put on the infinite horizon of God's presence. The director has the opportunity to listen and guide through the rough waters; to offer affirmation and hope; to pray for and with those who have felt so alienated and alone in a sea of Christian married couples.

You may be excited to try spiritual direction but how do you find and choose someone trained in this area? A call to your local parish, retreat houses or centers for spiritual development will be obvious first resources. Spiritual Directors International, a professional organization, has a directory for every state and region.[1] Do not assume that all spiritual directors are priests or professed religious. Formation programs all over the world are training laypeople from all walks of life.

Spiritual direction provides the participant spouse with a comforting, reassuring place to fulfill her need to talk about what is happening to her spiritually. The director is ethically bound to hold everything in confidence. The individual thus comes to a safe place to disclose whatever lies close to the heart. It is a place to grieve and cry over what she may never experience in the marital relationship. It is a place to question and learn about God's will. It is a place to learn about faith development and to understand the many changes that happen over time. It is a place of affirmation, learning to trust, a place to reshape images of God. Finally, it is a place to satisfy the hunger and need for companionship at the core of all who walk alone in faith.

CHAPTER SEVEN

THE JOURNEY AHEAD

"Different people have different roads to follow and we must go with others on the best road for them, not the one upon which we are most comfortable."[1] Morton Kelsey's advice on spiritual guidance looms great in my heart, and I include this quote to leave you with an important truth for the journey ahead. Outer evidence to the contrary aside, everyone walks a spiritual path. Some of us are just more intentional or obvious about it. The destination is the same (union with God) but how we travel there is diverse. Recognition, appreciation and encouragement of individual differences, in the end, constitute real love. Those of us who walk alone and walk together in marriage have the opportunity of experiencing this reality if we are less preoccupied with our spouse's spirituality and focus instead on our own calling from God.

Richard Gaillardetz says that marriage is "a daring promise...a most perilous undertaking, a journey fraught with risk."[2] When I hear young couples repeat their wedding vows, my throat constricts as they promise "for better or for worse" and "until death do us part." None of us knows what these vows will mean as we walk together through life. Pronouncements before God and everyone in a church do not guarantee living happily ever after. Yet there are still plenty of people who desire the commitment and welcome the chance to love another person for the long haul. Once again, the parallel journey into God strikes me with precise clarity. The many lessons we learn trying to live out the marriage covenant teaches and draws us into the Holy One, the source of all love. Our human imperfections affect that journey, but when we are committed to God, "for better or for worse...until death do us part," the bond becomes unbreakable. Growth will happen. We will never be alone. Solitude will become our place of love-making. The mystery of relationships will enchant and delight us. A strong foundation for family and children will be set. Friends and guides will hold our hands, listen to our hearts and walk the road with us.

During a youth retreat recently, someone asked me to explain why Jesus said that there is no marriage in heaven. "Sacraments are for those living on earth," I told the group. I explained, as best I could, that union with God replaces all human need for others. Seeing that the teens were a bit upset about this, I decided to venture a bit further. I told them that everyone in heaven will be so in love with God that we will all be united in one very big relationship. "So, Johnny, it will be like you and I are married." A look of horror crossed his handsome sixteen-year-old face, and I quickly saw that I had better do some more explaining!

I challenge you to reflect a bit more about the "no marriage in heaven" comment. What statement was Jesus making about the ultimate love relationship, the eternal marriage? We cannot imagine everlasting union. We cannot visualize living anywhere but on this beautiful blue orb called Earth, walking with the ones we love. But if there really is only one love story, then the journey into God, alone and together, is well worth the effort and sacrifices demanded of such a wonderful and mysterious adventure.

JOURNAL REFLECTIONS AND PRAYER STARTERS

(For individual or group use)

CHAPTER ONE: GROWTH AND STAGNATION

JOURNAL REFLECTIONS:

What fears are preventing you from spiritual growth?

What resistance will you meet if you go public with your feelings about God?

What stage of spiritual growth are you currently in?

PRAYER STARTERS:

Loving God, help me to...

Faithful God, give me the courage to...

CHAPTER TWO: LONGING, LONELINESS AND LOVE

JOURNAL REFLECTIONS:

How have you channeled your longing for God?

When do you feel most alone and most lonely within your marital relationship?

Does the spiritual journey come between you and your spouse?

PRAYER STARTERS:

Creator of all relationships, fill my heart with love for...

Guardian of intimacy, protect and guide my relationship as I...

CHAPTER THREE: SOLITUDE AND COMMUNITY

JOURNAL REFLECTIONS:

How have you carved out times of solitude for your spiritual growth?

Do you feel the need for more togetherness or more solitude within your marriage?

How do you feel about participating alone in your faith community?

PRAYER STARTERS:

Divine beloved who calls me into solitude, walk with me as I...

Divine beloved who calls me into community, walk with me as I...

CHAPTER FOUR: MYSTERY AND RELATIONSHIPS

JOURNAL REFLECTIONS:

How has your relationship with your spouse changed over time?

Where is God on the relationship continuum: Stranger? Acquaintance? Friend? Intimate?

Has your relationship with God enhanced or divided your other relationships?

PRAYER STARTERS:

Source of all love, fill me with your...

Source of all love, forgive me for...

CHAPTER FIVE: CHILDREN AND FAMILY

JOURNAL REFLECTIONS:

How has your spiritual journey affected your family?

What struggles do you face as you integrate spirituality into your home?

How can you bring your interior changes to the exterior?

PRAYER STARTERS:

Center of my life, I lift these family concerns to you...

Center of my life, teach me to...

CHAPTER SIX: FRIENDS AND GUIDES

JOURNAL REFLECTIONS:

Whom do you talk to about your spiritual journey?

What do you find most difficult about spiritual friendships?

Do you feel the need for spiritual direction? If you have a spiritual director: How does spiritual direction help you grow?

PRAYER STARTERS:

Holy Friend, enter into my relationships and show me...

Holy Friend, bless and nurture...

NOTES

PART ONE: WALKING ALONE

1. Thomas Merton, *The Seven Storey Mountain*, New York: Harcourt Brace, 1948.

CHAPTER ONE: GROWTH AND STAGNATION

1. Ronald B. Adler, Lawrence B. Rosenfelt, Russell F. Proctor II, *Interplay: The Process of Interpersonal Communication* (New York: Oxford University Press, 2004).
2. Ronald Rolheiser, *The Struggle for Generative Discipleship: From Wrestling with the Devil to Wrestling with God*, recording available through Los Angeles Religious Education Congress, www.recongress.org.
3. Rolheiser.
4. James W. Fowler, *Stages of Faith*, New York: HarperCollins, 1981.

CHAPTER TWO: LONGING, LONELINESS AND LOVE

1. Ronald Rolheiser, *The Restless Heart: Finding Our Spiritual Home* (New York: Doubleday, 2004), pp. 15–38.
2. Saint Augustine, *The Confessions of St. Augustine*, John K. Ryan, trans. (New York: Doubleday, 1960), p. 1.
3. Saint John of the Cross, *The Collected Works of St. John of the Cross*, Kieran Kavanaugh, O.C.D., and Otilio Rodriguez, O.C.D., trans. (Washington, D.C.: ICS, 1979). Saint Teresa of Avila, *The Collected Works of St. Teresa of Avila*, Kieran Kavanaugh, O.C.D., and Otilio Rodriguez, trans. (Washington, D.C.: ICS, 1987).
4. Caryll Houselander, *The Reed of God* (London: Sheed and Ward, 1976).
5. For further reading on this application of the paschal mystery, see Ronald Rolheiser, *The Holy Longing: The Search for a Christian Spirituality* (New York: Doubleday, 1999), pp. 141–166.

CHAPTER THREE: SOLITUDE AND COMMUNITY

1. James Finley, *The Awakening Call: Fostering Intimacy with God* (Notre Dame, Ind.: Ave Maria, 1984), p. 78.

2. For more information about the Los Angeles Religious Education Congress, see www.recongress.org.

3. Ideas are taken from many books, articles and tapes provided by the Carmelite monks of the Spiritual Life Institute located at Nada Hermitage, P.O. Box 219, Crestone, CO 81131. More information is available on their Web site: www.spirituallifeinstitute.org.

4. To subscribe, use the above Web site address and click on *Desert Call: Contemplative Christianity and Vital Culture* or contact the Spiritual Life Institute, P.O. Box 219, Crestone, CO 81131.

5. William McNamara, *Christian Humanism*, set of six audiotapes, available through the Spiritual Life Institute, P.O. Box 219, Crestone, CO 81131. These concepts also appear in William McNamara, *The Human Adventure: The Art of Contemplative Living* (New York: Amity House, 1974), pp. 27–43.

6. McNamara, *The Human Adventure*, pp. 27–43.

7. William McNamara, O.C.D., *Mystical Passion: The Art of Christian Loving* (New York: Amity House, 1977).

8. More information about the Cursillo Movement can be obtained by writing the National Cursillo Movement, P.O. Box 210226, Dallas, TX 75111, or by visiting its Web site: www.natl-cursillo.org.

PART TWO: WALKING TOGETHER

1. Richard Rohr makes this point in many books and tapes available through the Center for Action and Contemplation, 1705 Five Points Road, Albuquerque, NM 87195 or by going to their Web site: www.cacradicalgrace.org.

CHAPTER FOUR: MYSTERY AND RELATIONSHIPS

1. Most of this section comes from many sources on interpersonal communication theory. For further reading, I suggest Gerald R. Miller and Mark Steinberg, *Between People* (Chicago: Science Research Associates, 1975), pp. 196–226.

2. For specific reading in this area, I suggest Joseph Glynn, O.C.D., *The Eternal Mystic: St. Teresa of Avila, The First Woman Doctor of the Church* (New York: Vantage, 1982), or William Johnston, *Mystical Theology: The Science of Love* (New York: Orbis, 1995).

3. Guided Imagery with Music retreats are given every year through the Personal Growth Project. Contact Sister Joan King, 5725 Paradise Drive, Corta Madera, CA 94925.

CHAPTER FIVE: CHILDREN AND FAMILY

1. Richard Rohr, O.F.M., and Paula D'Arcy, *Spirituality for the Two Halves of Life* (audio) (Cincinnati: St. Anthony Messenger Press, 2005).

2. *Vatican Council II: The Conciliar and Post Conciliar Documents*, Austin Flannery, O.P., ed. (New York: Costello, 1975), p. 728.

CHAPTER SIX: FRIENDS AND GUIDES

1. For more information about Spiritual Directors International, please go to www.sdiworld.org.

CHAPTER SEVEN: THE JOURNEY AHEAD

1. Morton T. Kelsey, *Companions on the Inner Way: The Art of Spiritual Guidance* (New York: Crossroad, 1963), p. 203.

2. Richard R. Gaillardetz, *A Daring Promise: A Spirituality of Christian Marriage* (New York: Crossroad, 2002), p. 9.